STILL WORM

ASHLEY YANG-THOMPSON

©2025 Ashley Yang-Thompson
All Rights Reserved
Published in the United States
www.bateaupress.org

ISBN: 978-1-7345166-9-2

Book layout by Mckinsey Carroll
mckinseycarroll.com

Photos on back cover and p. 4 by Guzman

All artwork unless otherwise mentioned by Ash Yang-Thompson

Bateau can function due to the dedicated and hardworking students found at College of the Atlantic. Shout out to every one of those wonderful people.
www.coa.edu

the Sylvia Beach of the 21st century ←

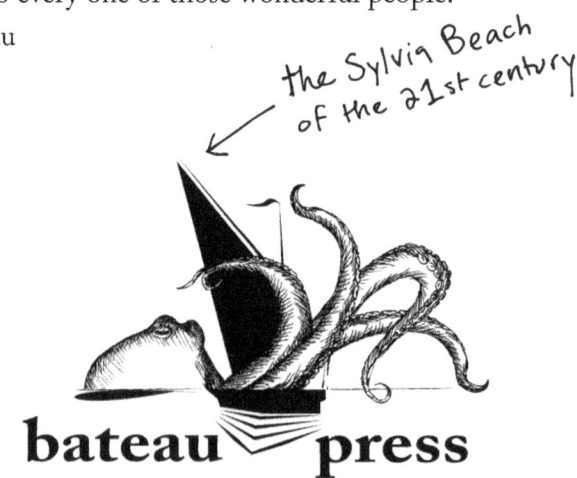

ADVANCED PRAISE
for *Still Worm*

Ashley Yang-Thompson writes with a rare freedom and wildness of thought. Part manifesto, part confession, part satire, part religious text, ruthlessly honest and original, *Still Worm* is a must-read for any artist or writer seeking to make sense out of this strange thing that we do.

—*Mikko Harvey*, author of *Let the World Have You*

The ultimate romantic gesture is to touch something living more than you touch your phone," writes Ashley Yang-Thompson in her winning debut collection *Still Worm*. Melding poetry, essay, cultural criticism, and barbaric yawp-filled artistic exhortation, Yang-Thompson's book refuses definition, in the service of being supremely readable and, in its own idiosyncratic way, revelatory. If you let it, this book will change you.

—*Jeff Alessandrelli*, director of *Fonograf Editions*

Read *Still Worm* and you might just "experience cow-like bliss" or even more remarkably "learn to poop without your phone." I can't say I achieved either, but I was reminded that the world doesn't need my achievements, "what it needs is to be loved better." The flesh walrus will show you how.

—*Kiera O'Brien*

This tender, obscene treatise is a linguistic evisceration. Yang-Thompson undoubtedly belongs in a canon that needs no blurb.
—*Adrian Ruth Williams*, author of *Batsong, rehearsals for an audioplay*

Vulnerable and tender as the earthworm, Yang-Thompson makes me question if it's real or cake; am I Artist or artist under Empire? A savage wordsmith, who will force you into introspection — when I also just wanted to browse for clogs online.

—*Carolyn Hugh*, author of *The Fortunes of Jaded Women*

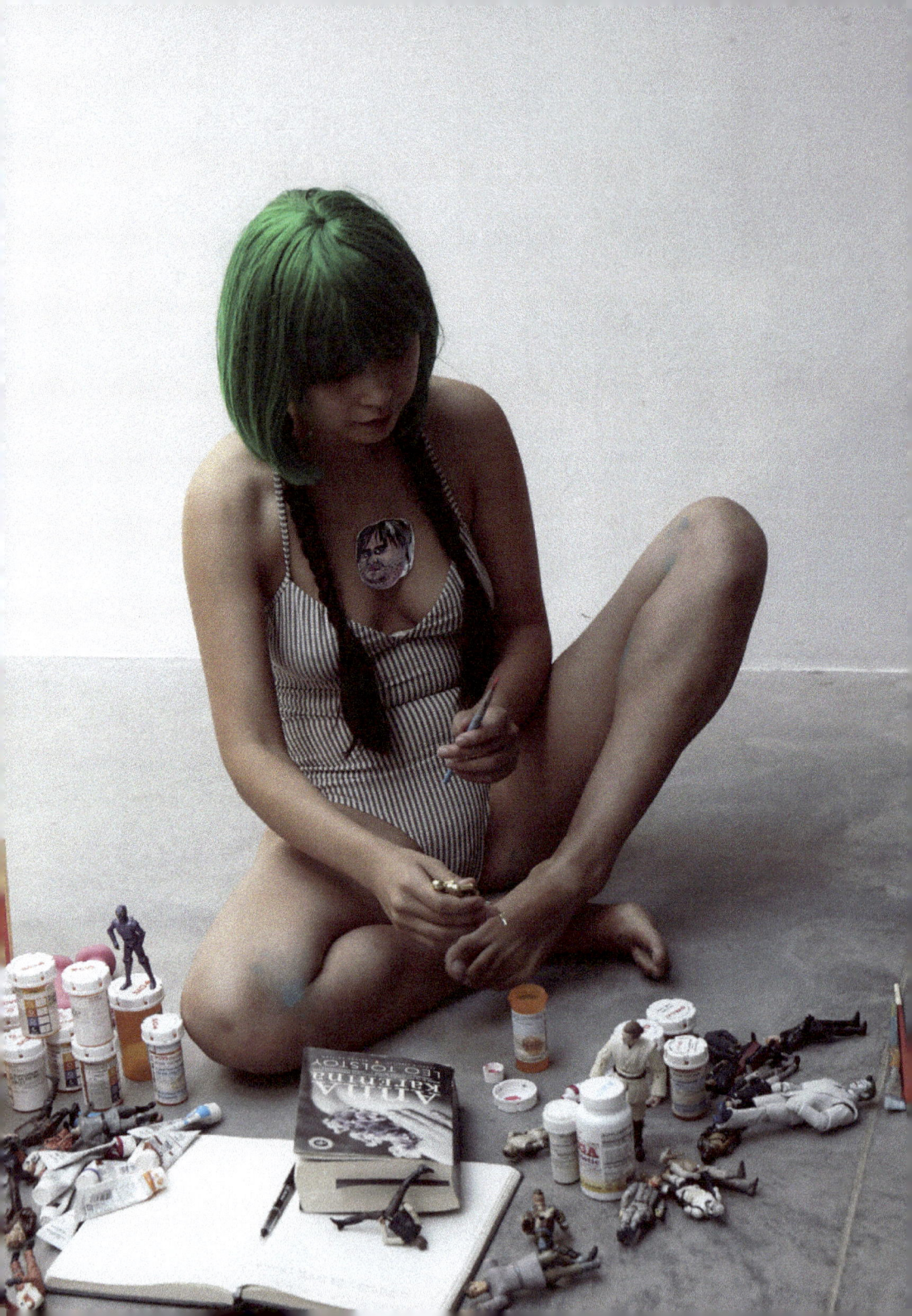

Ye have made your way from the worm to man,
and much within you is still worm.

– Friedrich Nietzsche, *Thus Spoke Zarathustra*

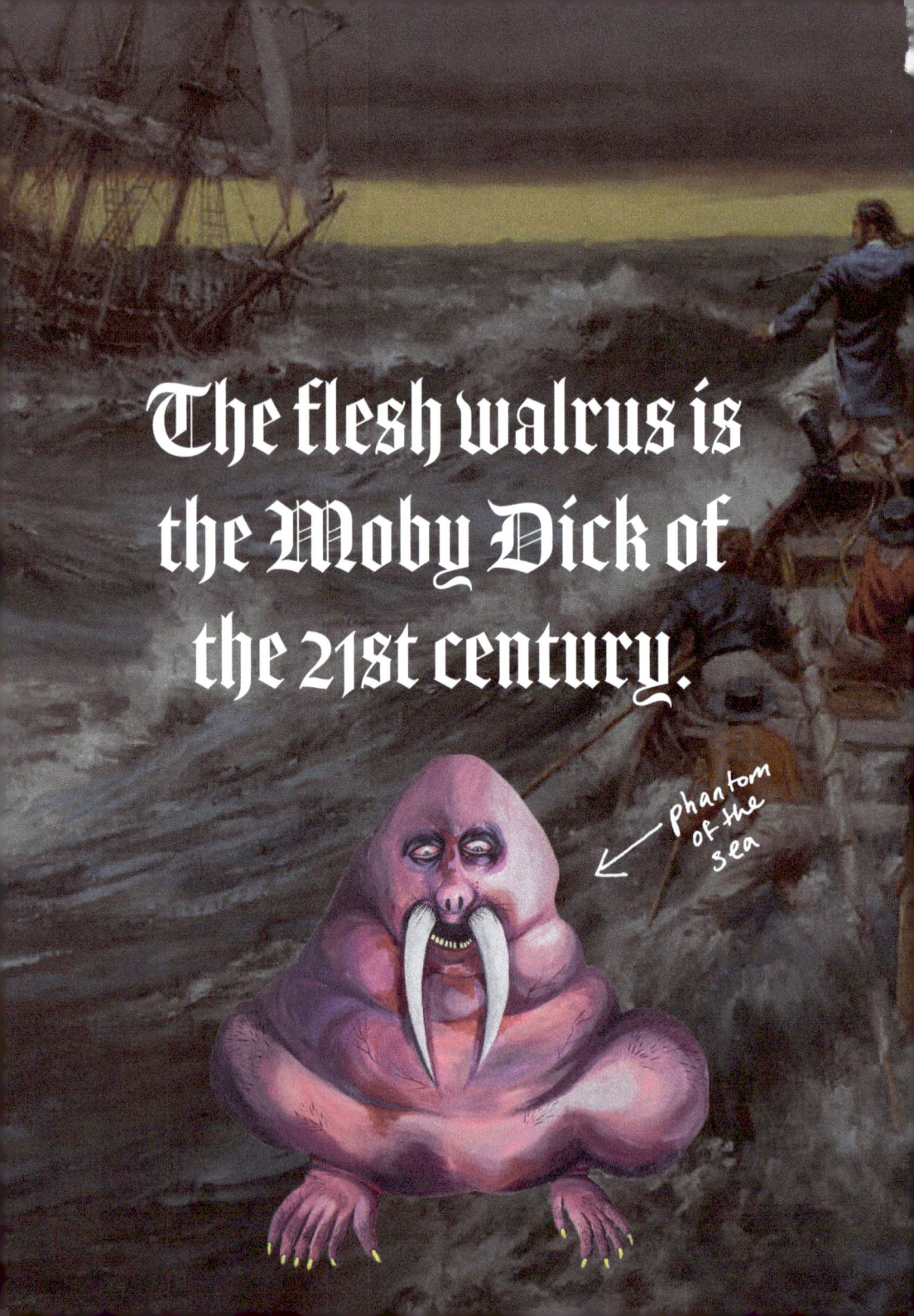

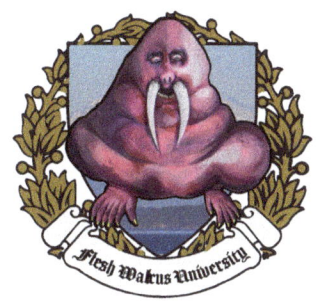

The ~~highly unprofessional~~ Pedagogical Philosophy of Ash Yang-Thompson

WHICH IS IN A PERPETUAL
STATE OF FLUX

BECAUSE LIFE RESISTS
COMPREHENSION

OR

I DO, I UNDO, I REDO

In homage to *My Struggle* by Karl Ove Knausgård

It is my pedagogical practice to enter the classroom
in a sleek yet utilitarian diaper made out of the walrus
blubber I have had liposuctioned out of my haunches.

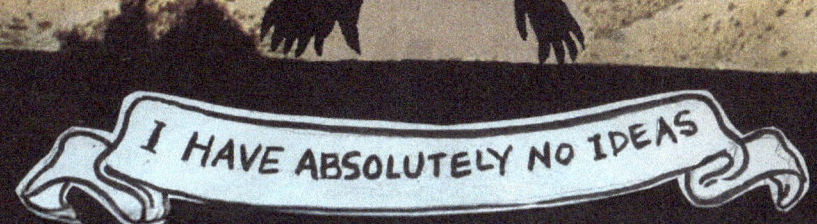

The Independent Voice of the Visual Arts

November 1984 $2.50/£1.75

HOW DO YOU STAY IN YOUR SKIN?

WORM HOUSE 40

THE ANGER FEELS LIKE WATER. LIKE IT'S RISING. MY BLOOD IS BOILING.

VOLCANIC FEELING

A WORK OF ART IS A SNAKESKIN PINNED TO THE WALL. A LIFETIME OF DEDICATION TO SHEDDING YOUR SKIN.

LIVING IS THE WORK OF ART. WHAT IF WE EMBRACED EVERY CHANGE OF PHASE? NOT GOOD NOT BAD JUST DIFFERENT.

NO FUSS

IF YOU HAVE 5 MINUTES TO SPARE

I JUST WANT TO BE A GOOD TRICK DOG

BANNED EMOTION

STAY UP TO DATE ON RESENTMENTS

A work of art is a snake skin pinned to the wall.

The object is the artifact, the residue, the bowel movements of the living, breathing thing which is Art.

Being an artist is a privilege. Never complain about being an artist. You have the gift of becoming fluent in your native tongue. There are over 7,000 dialects in this world, and not one of them is your native tongue. Your natural language does not exist yet; your task is to uncover the palimpsest of the soul.

Everyone is born under systems that cloud reality with prescribed thoughts and the invasive belief that anybody who's anybody must fit into a one-size-fits-nobody glass slipper.

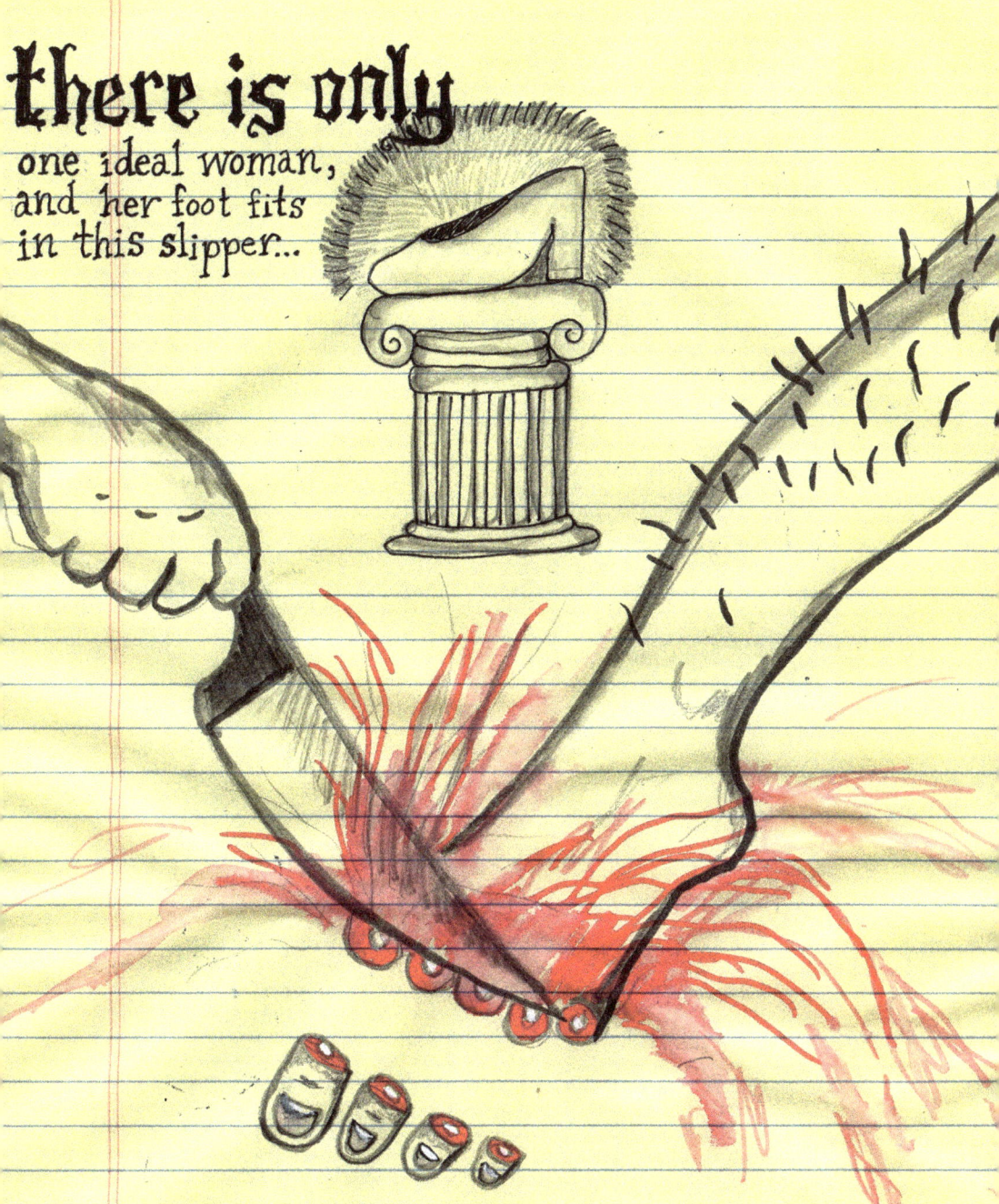

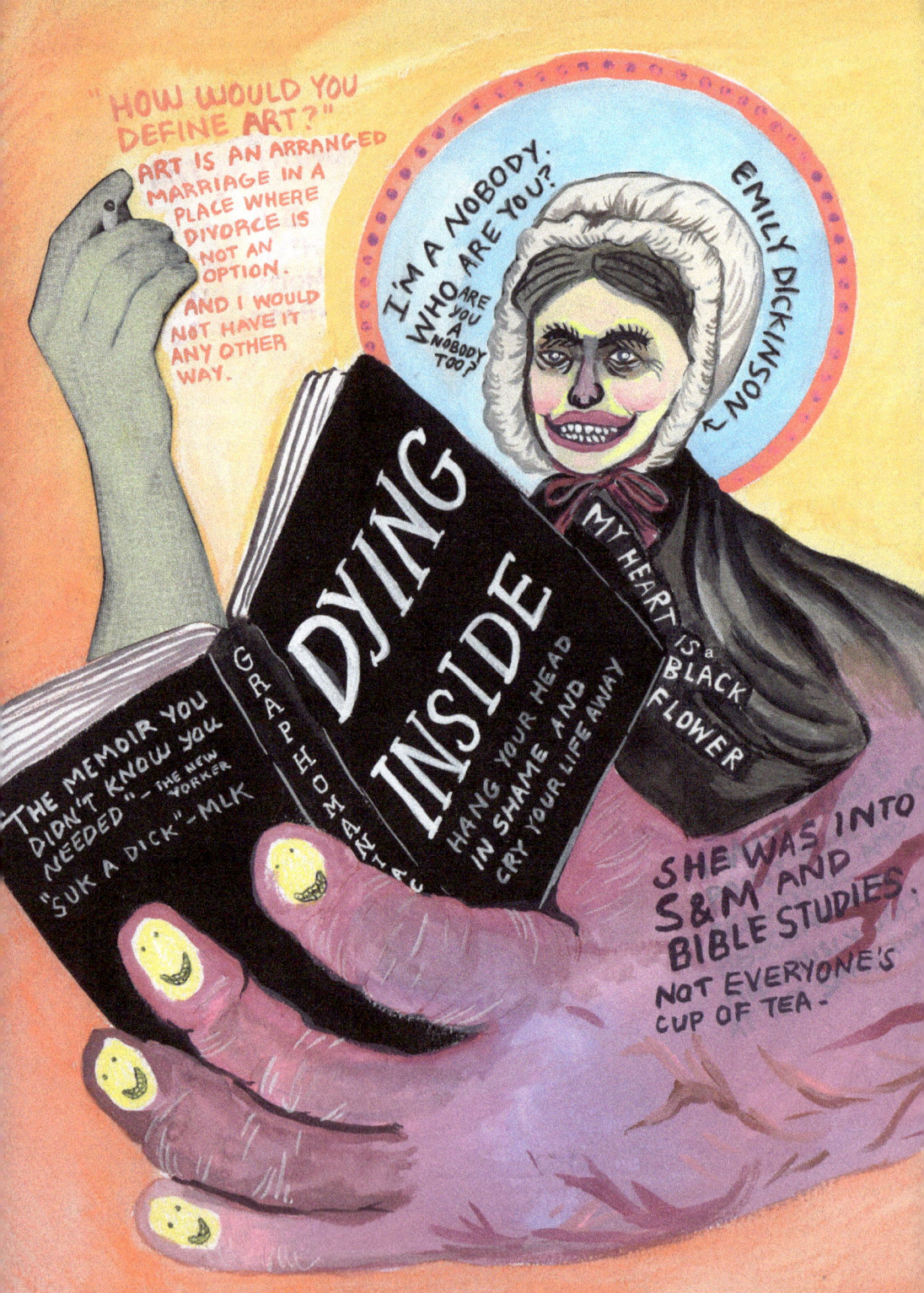

Be a nobody! As Emily Dickson said,

I'm Nobody! Who are you?
Are you – Nobody – too?
Then there's a pair of us!
Don't tell! they'd advertise – you know!
How dreary – to be – Somebody!
How public – like a Frog –
To tell one's name – the livelong June –
To an admiring Bog!

Poop is a complete metaphor for the natural cycles that determine art and life. Being an art-doer is peristalsis; it is the process of intake, assimilation, and elimination as we digest every moment of our life.

As soon as you begin to make art, you are burdened with the idea of what art should look like. We cannot control the look and timeliness of our inevitable defecations. Whether you come up with constipated pebbles, violent diarrhea, or a well-formed banana with the consistency of toothpaste, it is not a moral issue. The same is true for the residue of art. Get rid of value systems, and anything is possible.

(It is worth noting that trees also experience constipation; in the same way that a tree's rings show ample growth in an ideal climate, and atomized growth during drought, you are not to blame for burnout, exhaustion, defeat, and despair. Sometimes, oftentimes, art is a trudge. Try to be a happy Sisyphus.)

Try your dumbest ideas.

We are experimenting, researching, learning and unlearning. Making mistakes is poetic action.

As my dear friend Tabitha Nikolai once said,

The dumbest ideas often carry the tag of oppression.

> `i farted and it was not right`

NOBEL PRIZE-WINNING POEM

I choose the food,
my intestines do the work,
and every day my anus delivers
ephemeral, anti-capitalist Art.

Make whatever is necessary to you, and maybe it will be necessary to somebody else. Abolish the word "work" from your vocabulary. Work is the practice of whipping oneself in order to become master. Do not make "work." Work and productivity are antithetical to art.*

Self-optimization is anti-life. The pressure to perform is what fuels the fire of everything that is destructive to you. Art happens outside of mechanical living, it happens when you are going nowhere, looking like a fool, pleasing nobody, frustrated, fed up, wandering, and wasting time.

There is no art in rushing.

*I'm using hyperbolic language to express the idea that work is *not* an inherent virtue. Your work is to be present for your life.

HOUSE WORM

49 NOBODY HOME

RAIN RAIN GO AWAY... WANDERING IN THE WILDERNESS, NOT LOST, BUT NOT YET READY TO RECLAIM THEIR PLACE IN THE WORLD, TRYING TO GET THEIR SHIT TOGETHER...

SOMETHING THE ENERGY IS NOT AS BIG AS THE AMBITION

DEPRESSION IS A SYMPTOM OF GROWTH said the self-help book

I need a vacation from my brain

TIRED TIRED TIRED
HUNGRY HUNGRY HUNGRY
LONELY LONELY LONELY
BORED BORED BORED BORED
I GET UP AND I LIE DOWN.
I FALL TO MY KNEES IN SURRENDER
AND I ASCEND TO GREAT HEIGHTS.
I FEEL GOD AND THEN I FORGET HER.
I FEEL CONNECTED AND I FEEL
UTTERLY ALONE.
I FEEL EMPTY AND I FEEL
FULFILLED.
THE WATER FREEZES, BOILS,
AND EVAPORATES.
THERE IS A TIME
FOR EVERYTHING.

NO GOD IN RUSHING

Wake up! Don't look at your phone!

So much is happening in the world, or could be happening. Straightforward representation is not my aim, the world has no need to be represented: here it is, all around us, all the time. What it needs is to be loved better.

The ultimate romantic gesture is to touch something living more than you touch your phone.

<u>One day you wake up and everything is interesting.</u>
You run past your neighbor's house for the hundreth time,
You look up at the trees that have always been there,
 and what you see delights you.
The world appears as if it is breathing, and you are woven into
that aliveness. You are alert, you are paying attention,
and everything sings along with the song that is always going on,
the tune that carried you into being. You read your favorite magazine
while eating breakfast, you overhear a conversation at the coffee shop,
you look at the contents of your trash as if they are clues planted for
you by the benevolent-puppet-master-at-large. You've glimpsed the thread
you've been following all along, and it's terribly exciting.
Your pangs of hunger make you laugh, your exhaustion makes you gentle,
you ask the man at the register of your local Chinese dollar store why
 hanging an eggplant on the front door brings good luck and he delivers
the line: What you believe becomes true for you.
This day is an ordinary day. Nothing momentous has happened to you.
You didn't just win an award or land your dream job or make a pile of
dough. You didn't get whisked away by a beautiful and inspiring stranger,
nobody noticed your peculiar brand of genius. You didn't get a letter from
a friend or make peace with your mother or have a breakthrough at work.
You didn't even get one new Worm House subscriber. Literally nothing
interesting is happening but today your rough edges are rounded, you've
already been forgiven, you give a happiness that spreads, and all around
the world glows.

xoxo,
Your Local Nutcase

Do whatever it takes to *play profound*.

In the words of the modern dance choreographer Susan Rethorst,

Pleasure and rigor are not mutually exclusive. Rigor is misunderstood, too closely associated with the work ethic and with effort, will and vigor...

Pleasure is also of the intellect. Pleasure is a good thing. It means the heart is beating with curiosity. It means the spirit of a person is engaged. Such engagement can come from the reading of a difficult text as surely as it can come from basking in the sun. Different pleasures, but pleasures both. Pleasure is necessary to work. Pleasure need not imply laziness or sloth, but rather a form of openness – of play. Good art comes more from the play instinct than the work instinct.

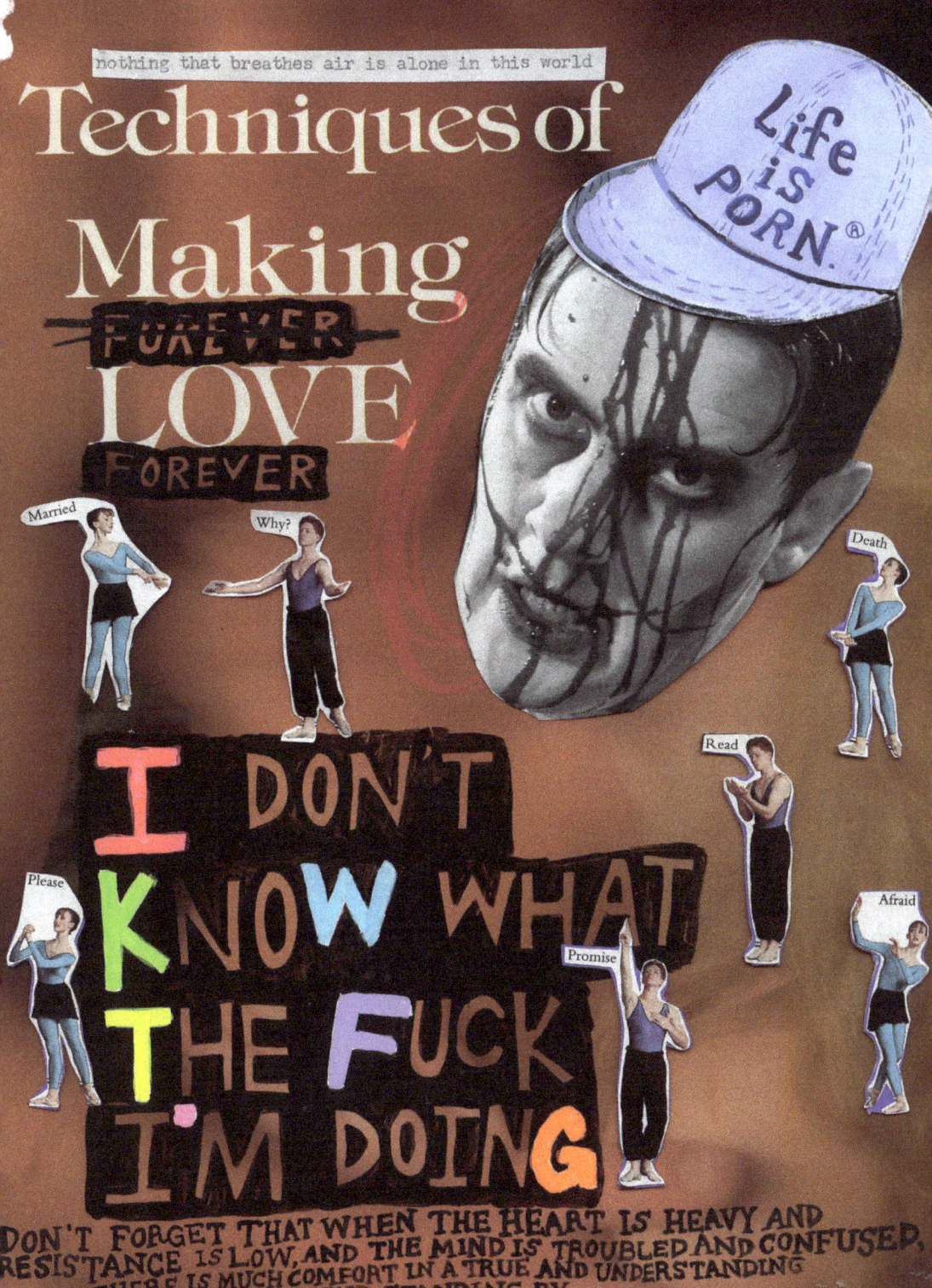

Do not be afraid to contradict yourself.

Contradicting oneself is one of the most fundamental, truthful things you can do. According to wave-particle theory, the foundation of the universe contradicts itself – it is not possible for something to be both a wave and a particle at the same time, yet that impossibility exists at the core of matter – if atoms are the building blocks of life, we are made of paradoxes.

By holding on to the tension of opposites, the third way, or *transcendent function* opens up.*

---

*I have a Jungian therapist.

What is poetry?

Poetry is the world highlighted.
Poetry is my native tongue.
Poetry is a process of becoming.
It is an intimate code.
Poetry is experience and experiments.
Experience peeled and chopped and blended into a smoothie.
It's all about proportions and ratios and experimentation.
I think trying to write the poem YOU want to write is like yelling at a seed to grow.
Poetry is a shy animal that requires persistant coaxing.
Poetry is learning to see that life is... *what?*

YOU MUST FEEL WHAT YOU HOPE TO MAKE OTHERS FEEL.

Do what is most difficult. Avoid tricks.
Poetry takes shape the way pain shapes your life.
Write the poem that saves your own life. The poem that will save your own life is the poem that shatters the frozen sea inside.
If you are Full of Shit, you are not alone. Most people suffer from emotional constipation.
Poetry is a smooth morning poop. It can also be a constipated pebble.

Everywhere you look, there is a poem waiting to happen. Stop waiting. You are the special occasion of your life.

Never judge a work of art by its defects.

My high school English teacher told me: lucky is another word for loved.

PERMISSION TO BE SCATTERED & SNARLED

Trillium is a wild perennial that resists domestication. If you remove this three petaled flower from its environment, it will be dead by the time you reach the front door.

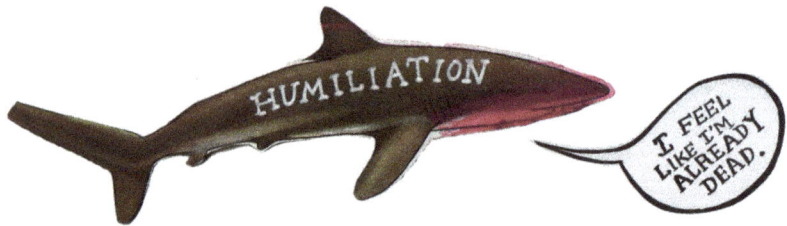

Great White sharks are notoriously absent in aquariums because they cannot survive in captivity. The few times aquariums have attempted to contain them, they exhibit symptoms not unlike my panic attacks – repeatedly banging their heads against their pellucid cage to the point of injury, refusing to eat, and losing their ability to swim.
Art is another one of these creatures.
You may be getting a "Master's" degree in art,
but do not be mistaken, you will never *master* art.

To paraphrase the poet Dean Young, art is an explosion, a hunger, a drive, a fright, a risk, a tantrum, a polar plunge, a grief, a gag joke, a divine defecation.

It is a momentary glimpse at something wild and free and utterly out of grasp.

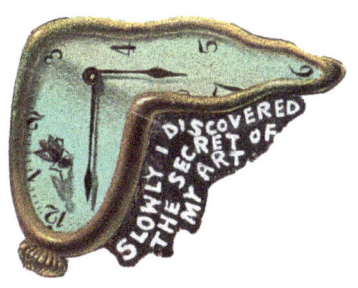

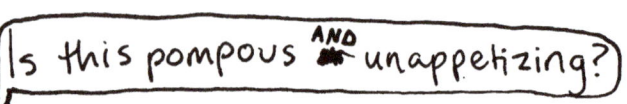

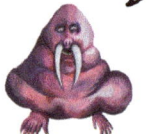

Flesh Walrus University
98% Acceptance Rate

Ash's Course Syllabus
ART69 – Resolving Psychic Flatulence

Cognitive Disobedience (and the Right To Be Lazy)

Instructor: Ash Yang-Thompson

Office: Case Study Coffee Roasters, Nossa Familia Coffee, Powell's "City of Books," et cetera. Loitering is a highly encouraged sociological survey of the infraordinary.

Availability: Available for spontaneous encounters

Phone: No phone. Please leave detailed notes with the employees at one of my office locations.

Email: There will be no emails in this class.

Location: This is not an online course — decaying meatsacks only.

Course Description

(to be read out loud with orotund intonation)

Uncreative writing. Non-editing. The Art of copying. Found poetry. Primal authenticity. Vexed queerness. Imperfectionism. Life as collage. Uncomfortable conversations as research. Question your identity. Lose track of yourself. Crack the husks of habit. Learn to poop without your phone. Fight to keep yourself engaged with other humans. Break things. Allow your brain to be broken. Unlearn something. Experience cow-like bliss. Experience the serenity of madness. Celebrate amateurism. Insist on the process of becoming. Become oatmeal (true story). Retire the word "work." Aesthetics as aisthesis. Practice being unlikable. Exhale. Learn to poop without your phone.

What would you be doing with your life if you were not trying to "succeed"?
What would it mean, on an emotional level,
to make work not the defining feature of our lives?
How could such a procedure be carried out?
What does it really mean to hold that everything fluctuates, and, being relational, changes its identity?
This is a class for experimental living.

We will operate under the following assumptions:
(1) Everything you need, you have.
(2) You have already made the art.
(3) Your discovery of how to write your book is your book.

THE MOST IMPORTANT NOTE
(until we abandon superlatives):
I prefer the term "facilitator" to instructor.

My intention is not to inform but to create an active and collaborative space.
Like you, I know nothing.
Like you, I pursue knowledge anyway.
Nothing about this class is absolute —
we will operate under an antidisciplinary and unfinished system.
This syllabus, like water, is jerking off.

Course Outcomes/Learning Objectives

To give up on being miserable.
To stop trying to improve oneself.
To decolonize our emotional lives.
To contradict oneself.
To exercise cognitive disobedience.
To do whatever it takes to internalize art as a form of play and not commit suicide.
To resist the urge to make one's creations more beautiful.
To resist the goal-oriented tautological present
(I don't know what that means, either. But I want to find out.)
To resist the tyranny of email.
To reject normative protocols of canonization and value and cease to contribute labor power at the proper tempo.
To refuse comfort, predictability and safety.
To deliberately seek out the difficult, the unknown, the ambiguous and unpredictable.

To look upon the garbage person as if they were a famous artist, and vice versa.
To find solidarity with your intellectual soulmates.
To eat real bread and give up on delusional love.

Course Prerequisites

You must be an autodidact and have an overwhelming desire to be here.
You must be willing to take a nap when tired.

Suggested Materials

piñata (homemade or store bought)
3 Health Mounds* a day
Uses of the Erotic: The Erotic As Power, Audre Lorde
On Photography, Susan Sontag
On Women, Susan Sontag
On (Not) Sleeping With Your Students, Amia Srinivasan
Taking Female Students Seriously, Adrienne Rich
Teaching to Transgress, bell hooks
Cruising Utopia, Jose Estaban Munoz
In Praise of Idleness, Bertrand Russell
Healing as Killing, Byung-Chul Han

*More on that later.

No Technology

There is a zero tolerance policy for smartphones within a half-mile radius. Students who ignore this policy will be required to drown their devices in a fountain of balloon-breasts squirting Fuji water.

Major Assignments

Make Bad Art

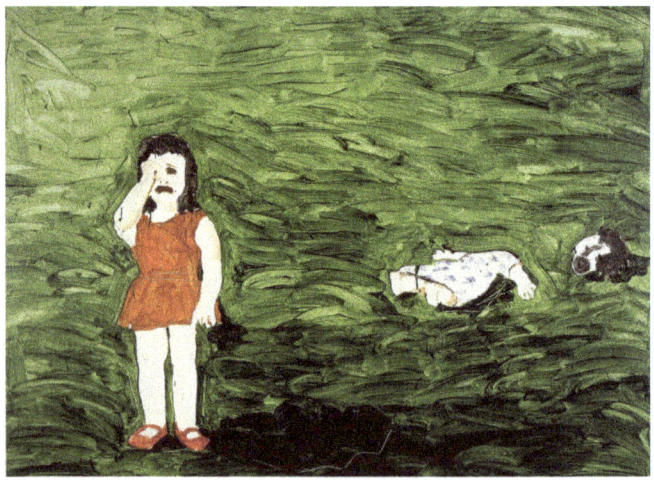

Neil Jenny, Girl and doll, 1969 (Neil Jenny is inexplicably represented by Gagosian Gallery).

Bad taste is real taste, of course, and good taste is the residue of someone else's privilege.

– Dave Hickey

You must practice being stupid dumb unthinking empty. Then you will be able to DO, wrote Sol Lewitt in a letter to Eva Hesse. Trying one's dumbest ideas is far from a fatuous imperative. By turning towards and taking seriously one's own rejected thoughts, we ask the question, who decides what's dumb (or bad or hideously ugly)? *Our dumbest ideas often carry the tag of oppression.**

As we develop our theory and praxis of Bad Art, ancillary texts may include: Jean DuBuffet's *Anticultural Positions*, John Cage's *Lecture on Nothing*, Dave Hickey's *Air Guitar*, and Julia Kristeva's defiant allegiance to abjection in *Powers of Horror*. Students will also be asked to share examples of works that have truly altered their worlds.

We will celebrate failure in the following categories:

1. Needs Validation
2. So Bad It's Good
3. Most Alarming Use of Color
4. Most Poorly Rendered Human/Animal/Creature
5. Least Abstract-y Abstract
6. Most Distorted Recognizable Object
7. Acid Trip Gone Wrong
8. Earnest But Still Bad
9. Most Self-Indulgent
10. Most Likely To Be Mistaken For Fan Fiction
11. Best Used As Kindling

*Tabitha Nikolai

12. Annoyingly Pretentious/Tumescent
13. I Know It's Bad But I Love It And Can't Explain Why
14. Ugly Like My/Your Soul (but like in a good way)
15. Trying, but Truly Terrible
16. Trying Too Hard
17. Not Trying Hard Enough
18. Nice Try: This Is Actually Good
19. Good And Bad Are Labels. All Language Is Meaningless. Just Like Life.
20. Can't Stop, Won't Stop, Please Stop
21. But Look How Big/Long/Tall It Is!
22. At Least Your Mom Loved It
23. Work Most Likely To Be Mistaken For That Of A Precocious Child
24. Participation Trophy
25. So Different!
26. Makes me laugh so hard I cry!
27. Everything You Touch Turns To Gold. Except This.

Commonplace Book

A commonplace book is the lovechild of a research log and a scrapbook. Whatever stirs you – whatever passages or images or facts or recipes or lyrics that light up the mind with corruscating effervescence – belong in this book. A commonplace book is a florilegium of work that is necessary and dear to one's heart. The process of choosing, ordering, reordering, and juxtaposing research is an original aesthetic act akin to making a collage or recording a song which samples other artists. Students will be asked to keep this book with them at all times — to make it an extension of their own skin, and add to it on a daily basis.

Possible themes:

FAILURE	ABJECTION
IMAGINATION	HEALTH
CENSORSHIP	TIME
IDENTITY	NATURE
OBSCENITY	WASTE
RESONANCE	PRETENTIOUSNESS
TECHNOLOGY	WHAT THE FUCK?*
MORALITY	AUTOBIOGRAPHY
GUILT	PRIVACY
LOSS	ADDICTION
BETRAYAL	ANGER
DOUBT	ANGST
FEAR	ANXIETY
LONELINESS	OBSESSION
DEPRESSION	WHY AM I ME AND NOT YOU?
DESPAIR	AMBIGUITY
MONSTROSITY	EMBODIMENT
BEAUTY	RAPTURE

*(anything that might inspire the aforementioned idiom)

Virginia Woolf, Ralph Waldo Emerson, Henry David Thoreau, Michel de Montaigne and countless other writers kept commonplace books.

Constructing a Personal Canon

You are a fool to read classics because you are told to and not because you like them.

– Ezra Pound

What remains true? What does it mean for something to be "timeless?" What makes a poem so good that it delivers with each recitation, and carries weight and meaning across a lifetime? A poem that transforms as you transform. All of literature is our creative inheritance. Each student will construct their own personal canon based on the artists and writers whose work resonates with their inner authority.

In every work of genius we recognize our own rejected thoughts; they come back to us with a certain alienated majesty.

– Ralph Waldo Emerson

Students will list every book they have ever read, and keep a continuous litany of what they are reading either on a google doc or their website a la Tao Lin. We will discuss how every author who has exploded our minds and given birth to ideas is an inheritor as well as an originator. Your personal canon will

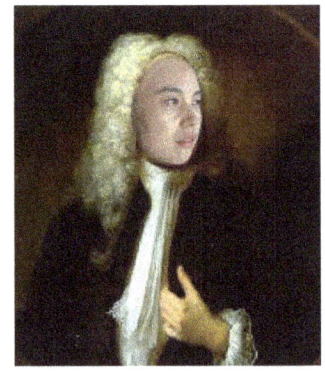

center around creating or discovering a tradition that is supportive to the way YOU, and YOU ALONE, make stuff.

Writing Exercises

First thought, best thought.

– Allen Ginsberg

Flesh Walrus University© focuses on poetry as the practice of praising the causal everydayness of our lives. We will find inspiration in ancient Japanese Haikus, Allen Kaprow's Happenings, Audre Lorde's *Uses of the Erotic*, Susan Rethorst's concept of *Play Profound*, and the work of the New York School Poets.

Prompts:
- Write a memoir where every line begins with "I remember…" (after Joe Brainard's *I Remember*)
- Write a poem called "How to be Perfect" (after Ron Padget's *How to be Perfect*)
- Create a one-minute sculpture (After Erwin Wurm's *One-minute Sculptures*)
- Write a poem during your lunch break
- Write a poem on an ephemeral surface (such as a scrap of toilet paper or the back of a receipt)
- Create a zine out of collaged screen shots (after Max Ernst's *Surrealist Novel in Collage*)
- Write a ransom note

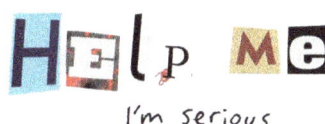

Collaboration, community, and play are encouraged. For example, if a student feels stuck or tired of writing their "I remember" memoir, they are invited to ask a classmate (or the grocery store clerk or their mom) to take over. We will write to amuse each other.

We emphasize making over revision. We will discuss letters, diaries, and found art – words and forms that leave profound impressions but were authentically unintended to be "work."
What art do we make simply by existing?

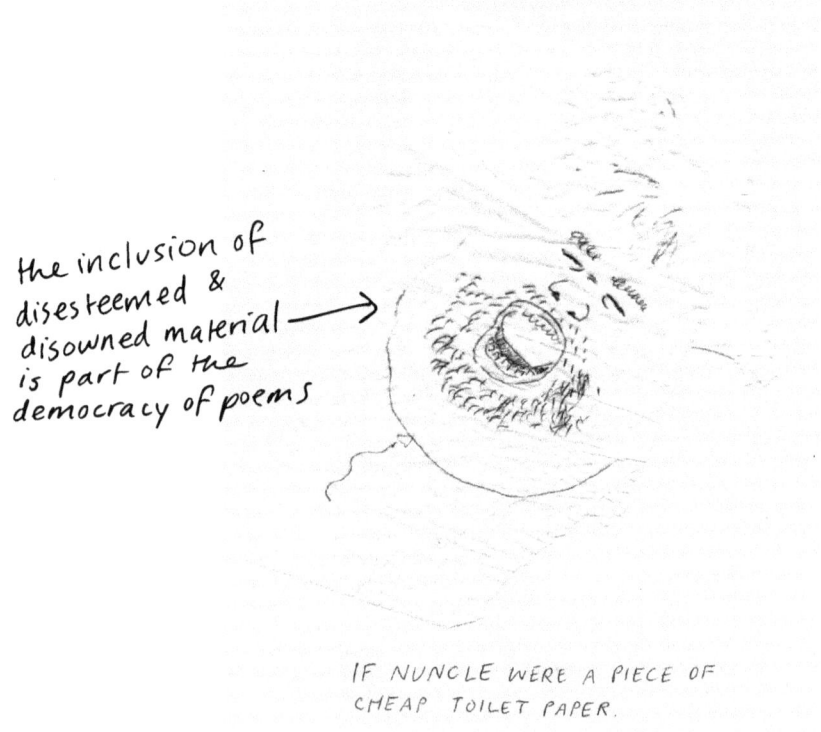

the inclusion of disesteemed & disowned material ⟶ is part of the democracy of poems

IF NUNCLE WERE A PIECE OF CHEAP TOILET PAPER.

Flexibility Statement

Please rip this syllabus to shreds and burn and/or stomp on the remains and create your own rigorous course of counter-knowledge.

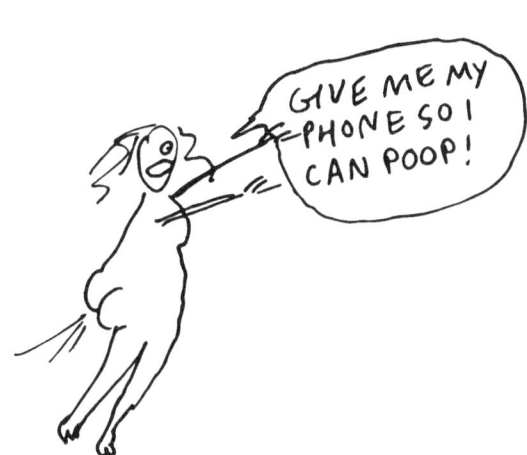

CREATIVE READING

*A book is a physical expansion of the human brain.
It is not an object to be treated lightly.*

– Mary Ruefle

*Despite every (failed) attempt to be the most well-read person
in the room at all times, I will never arrive at some final truth.
Reading complicates my sense of reality– fractures it– what was
once myopic blossoms into the kaleidoscopic.*

– my diary

For this class, all you need to do is bring something to read for approximately three minutes. This could be a few poems or an excerpt from an essay or a book or screenplay or fan-fiction or a recipe or pornography. I just ask that whatever you read resonates with you in a primal way – that this particular combination of words on paper matches the frequency of your pulse, has made you less full of shit, or has taught you how to live.

If that criteria sounds like a tall order, or if you have never experienced the sensuality of deep reading, don't worry, simply read something you are attracted to. As a class, we will operate under the assumption that each one of us is a god in the disguise of a beleaguered ~~MFA~~ student. I ask that when you are not reading, you practice listening.

Profound listening, which means that you give your classmates the restorative power of your undivided attention. I challenge you to refrain from the compulsion to multi-task, i.e. to experience less life by making the most out of every minute.

Reading is a form of art, a creative and collaborative act. Your interpretation of the text is uniquely yours and as valid as anybody else's. By bringing your whole self into the process of creative reading, you are uncovering new meanings. When you read a book, you learn more about yourself than the author – what you pay attention to is a mirror for your soul.

Final note:
Please do whatever it takes to look forward to this class.

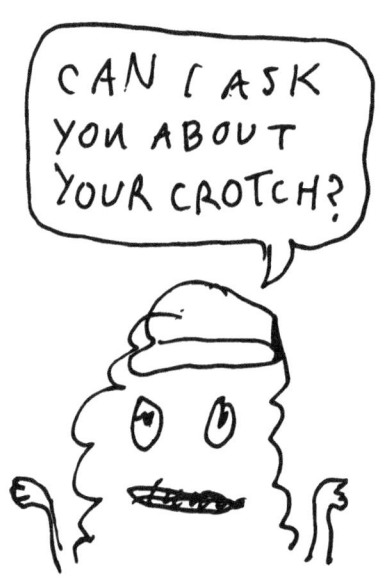

ONTOLOGICAL QUESTIONNAIRE

1. Do you want to know the unflattering truth about yourself?

   ☐ Yes ☐ No

2. Do you participate in sadistic beauty rituals?

   ☐ Yes ☐ No

3. Does your life cease to have meaning without a crush to metastasize?

   ☐ Yes ☐ No

4. What games are you playing with yourself?

   _____
   _____
   _____

5. Are you wretched?

   ☐ Yes ☐ No

6. Do you find yourself embodying the things you loathe in others?

   ☐ Yes ☐ No

7. Is learning and unlearning the perennial pattern of your life?

   ☐ Yes ☐ No

8. Do you ever return to things you once rejected?

   ☐ Yes ☐ No

9. In what ways have you been transformed?
   _____
   _____
   _____
   _____

10. What sort of weirdo are you?
    - [ ] I'm obsessed with raccoons
    - [ ] I often dress like a hamster
    - [ ] I paint with my poop
    - [ ] Asian cravin' bacon
    - [ ] I like to fart in elevators
    - [ ] Other (please specify) _____

11. Can the truth and fiction coalesce over time?
    - [ ] Yes
    - [ ] No

12. Where is the line dividing protecting one's solitude and self-alienation?
    _____
    _____
    _____

13. What does heartbreak feel like?
    _____
    _____
    _____

14. What constitutes good art? Bad art? Examples?

    _____
    _____
    _____

15. Are you a Deep Person?

    ☐ Yes   ☐ No

16. To what extent can and should we control our feelings?

    _____
    _____
    _____

17. What will matter to you in your dying moments?

    _____
    _____
    _____

18. How do you focus?

    _____
    _____
    _____

19. Do you wonder, "Am I failing at life?"

    ☐ Yes   ☐ No

20. When was the last time you teared up?

    _____
    _____
    _____

21. Is a new crush an old crush with a new face?

    ☐ Yes   ☐ No

22. Why do we fear what we desire?

    _____
    _____
    _____

23. What makes you feel high?

    _____
    _____
    _____

24. Good enough is better than an adrenaline rush. Agree or Disagree?

    ☐ Agree   ☐ Disagree

25. Do you chase everything you want away?

    ☐ Yes   ☐ No

26. Do you get what you want once you no longer want it?

    ☐ Yes   ☐ No

27. Does it comfort you to hear about other people's discomfort?

☐ Yes ☐ No

28. Have you slept enough?

☐ Yes ☐ No

29. Can you write if you're not reading?

☐ Yes ☐ No

30. When was the last time you were surprised?

_____
_____
_____

31. Is it healthy to devote your life to art?

☐ Yes ☐ No

32. Do you think you could recognize your own genitals?

☐ Yes ☐ No

33. Do you worry that you are not normal?

☐ Yes ☐ No

34. What do you owe other people?

_____
_____
_____

35. Have you learned to live with the mistakes you've made?

☐ Yes   ☐ No

36. Do you talk on the phone?

☐ Yes   ☐ No

37. Do you feel that we are 100% responsible for our own reality?

☐ Yes   ☐ No

38. Do you feel free?

☐ Yes   ☐ No

39. Do you like laser tag?

☐ Yes   ☐ No

40. What is Fine Art?

_____
_____
_____

41. Is it something that has to be esoteric and inconceivable and inaccessible or can it be what you felt last Tuesday?

    ☐ Esoteric and inconceivable   ☐ What you felt last tuesday

42. Is our internet search history an accurate mirror?

    ☐ Yes   ☐ No

43. Do you protect yourself from disappointment by expecting the worst case scenario?

    ☐ Yes   ☐ No

44. What does it mean to relax?

    _____
    _____
    _____

45. What do you do for fun?

    _____
    _____
    _____

46. Do you ever say, "Yass, Queen!"?

    ☐ Yass, Queen!   ☐ No

47. What feels urgent to you?

   _____
   _____
   _____

48. How do you tell if a poem is really good?

   ☐ I feel aroused

49. Is it good if it feels good to write it? Does it matter whether or not it is good or bad? Who decides what's good anyways?

   _____
   _____

50. What does it mean to be "in love"?

   ☐ Love is proof that time can accommodate eternity
   ☐ Love is an astonishing and overwhelming feeling
   ☐ Love is compulsively searching for a savior
   ☐ Love is a decision
   ☐ Love exceeds language
   ☐ Falling in love is falling out of love
   ☐ Other (please specify): _____
   ☐ Herpes is older than dinosaurs

51. Does redefining love negate past definitions of love?

   ☐ Yes ☐ No

52. How do you feed your longing for intimacy?

_____
_____
_____

53. Can you fart without holding back?

☐ Yes   ☐ No

54. How do you soothe yourself?

_____
_____
_____

55. In what ways do you sublimate anger?

_____
_____
_____

56. What was the last thing you asked Google?

_____

57. What is identity? Is it any more significant than a once-fashionable-now-faintly-stained article of clothing that we donate to Goodwill a few years later?

☐ Yes   ☐ No

58. Have you ever been in a cult?

☐ Yes   ☐ No

59. Who is your oldest friend?

_____

60. Do you use other people to regulate your nervous system?

    ☐ Yes ☐ No

61. What abides amid change?*

_____
_____
_____

62. What awed our ancestors?

_____
_____
_____

63. Do you keep putting life off?

    ☐ Yes ☐ No

64. Is food the only thing you look forward to?

    ☐ Yes ☐ No

65. Is the virtual real?

    ☐ Yes ☐ No

*Goethe's personal motto, according to James Hollis.

66. Who has seen you poop?

_____
_____

67. Is it normal to wish my heart would beat a little softer?

☐ Yes ☐ No

68. Is your life an exercise in constant humiliation?

☐ Yes ☐ No

69. Do you think of yourself as mundane?

☐ Yes ☐ No

70. How do you learn to outgrow your madness?

_____
_____
_____

71. Where do you stand on God?

_____
_____
_____

72. When was the last time you laughed so hard you cried?

_____
_____
_____

73. When was the last time you laughed so hard you peed your pants a little?

_____
_____
_____

74. How many times did you check your email today? _____

75. Do you remember anyone's phone number?

☐ Yes   ☐ No

76. Do you touch anything more than you touch your phone?

☐ Yes   ☐ No

77. Do you know anybody who has died from hot yoga?

☐ Yes   ☐ No

78. Can you poop in foreign bathrooms?

☐ Yes   ☐ No

79. What do you consider your purpose in life?

_____
_____
_____

80. Praise or blame, which is worse for the artist?

☐ Praise   ☐ Blame

81. Is inspiration for amateurs?

    ☐ Yes ☐ No

82. Can you imagine the terrible, unspeakable things someone has gone through?

    ☐ Yes ☐ No

83. Are you the kind of person who saves the best for last or do you dive right into the cream cheese frosting?

    ☐ Best for last   ☐ Cream cheese frosting

84. Are you adding something to the world?

    ☐ Yes ☐ No

85. How soon before bed should you stop drinking water?

    _____

86. Can anybody really not be interesting?

    ☐ Yes ☐ No

87. What was your earliest experience of music?

    _____
    _____

88. Are your desires aligned with your politics?

    ☐ Yes ☐ No

89. Do you think it's worth having a relationship where you can't be vulnerable? Can you be half-vulnerable, or is closeness all or nothing?

    ☐ Yes   ☐ No

90. How do you measure time?

    _____
    _____
    _____

91. What epiphanies, if any, have you had over the course of your life?

    _____
    _____
    _____

92. Do you look at your phone while you poop?

    ☐ Yes   ☐ No

93. How often do you think of suicide?

    _____
    _____
    _____

94. Do you feel your age? Older? Younger?

    ☐ I feel my age   ☐ I'm an old soul

    ☐ I'm 30 and still trying to look like an infantile anime porn boy

95. Are you lonely?

    ☐ Yes   ☐ No

96. Are you starving for connection?

    ☐ Yes   ☐ No

97. Are you using recreational drugs to salvage failing relationships?

    ☐ Yes   ☐ No

98. What do you do when you're at the intersection of hurt and boredom?

    _____
    _____
    _____

99. Are you regular?

    ☐ Yes   ☐ No

100. What do you think about muffins?

    _____
    _____
    _____

101. Why can't you be more like a microwave?

    _____
    _____
    _____

102. Can you feel the soft tickle of oblivion, or is it just me?

☐ The void is my friend   ☐ Shut up

103. What is the most beautiful thing you've ever seen?

_____
_____
_____

104. How often do you fake-smile? Fake laugh?

_____
_____
_____

105. What is information without wisdom?

_____
_____
_____

106. Does philosophizing ever make anyone happier?

☐ Yes   ☐ No

107. Is the point of life to be happy?

☐ Yes   ☐ No

108. What is left when all your projections are stripped away?

_____
_____
_____

109. Understanding is insanity for two, true or false?

    ☐ True   ☐ False

110. Do you feel like you've been chosen by God for a special task to accomplish here on Earth?

    ☐ Yes   ☐ No

111. How many tissues can be extracted from a tree? _____

112. How many licks does it take to get to a lifetime of sexual repression, or poop shame? _____

113. Do you ever wake up in the morning and feel like there's nothing in this life that you look forward to?

    ☐ Yes   ☐ No

114. Are you suffering from trickle down Catholic guilt?

    ☐ Yes   ☐ No

115. Would you like to dial the Spiritual Crisis Hotline?

    ☐ Yes   ☐ No

116. Do you make art to relieve yourself of your primordial insecurity?

    ☐ Yes   ☐ No

117. Are you beyond institutional validation?

    ☐ Yes   ☐ No

118. Are you waiting to be:

- [ ] Found
- [ ] Celebrated
- [ ] Crucified
- [ ] Discovered
- [ ] Turned on
- [ ] Rescued
- [ ] Eulogized
- [ ] Helped
- [ ] Resurrected
- [ ] Displayed over a fireplace

119. How do you inoculate yourself against the disease of disappointment?

_____
_____
_____

120. Are you a little bitch in your heart?

- [ ] Yes
- [ ] No

121. Do you need to be given permission?

- [ ] Yes
- [ ] No

122. Do you long for something to break up the plaque around your heart?

- [ ] Yes
- [ ] No

123. What makes you feel warm?

_____
_____
_____

124. If anything in the world could happen today, what would you want to happen?

_____
_____
_____

125. Do you ever fall to your knees and beg for forgiveness, without knowing precisely for what?

☐ Yes ☐ No ☐ Life is a vertiginous free-fall in which we stretch out our hands for support and find nothing but air running through our fingers.

126. What supports you when nothing supports you?*

---

*Carl Jung, as paraphrased by James Hollis in *Living with Borrowed Dust*

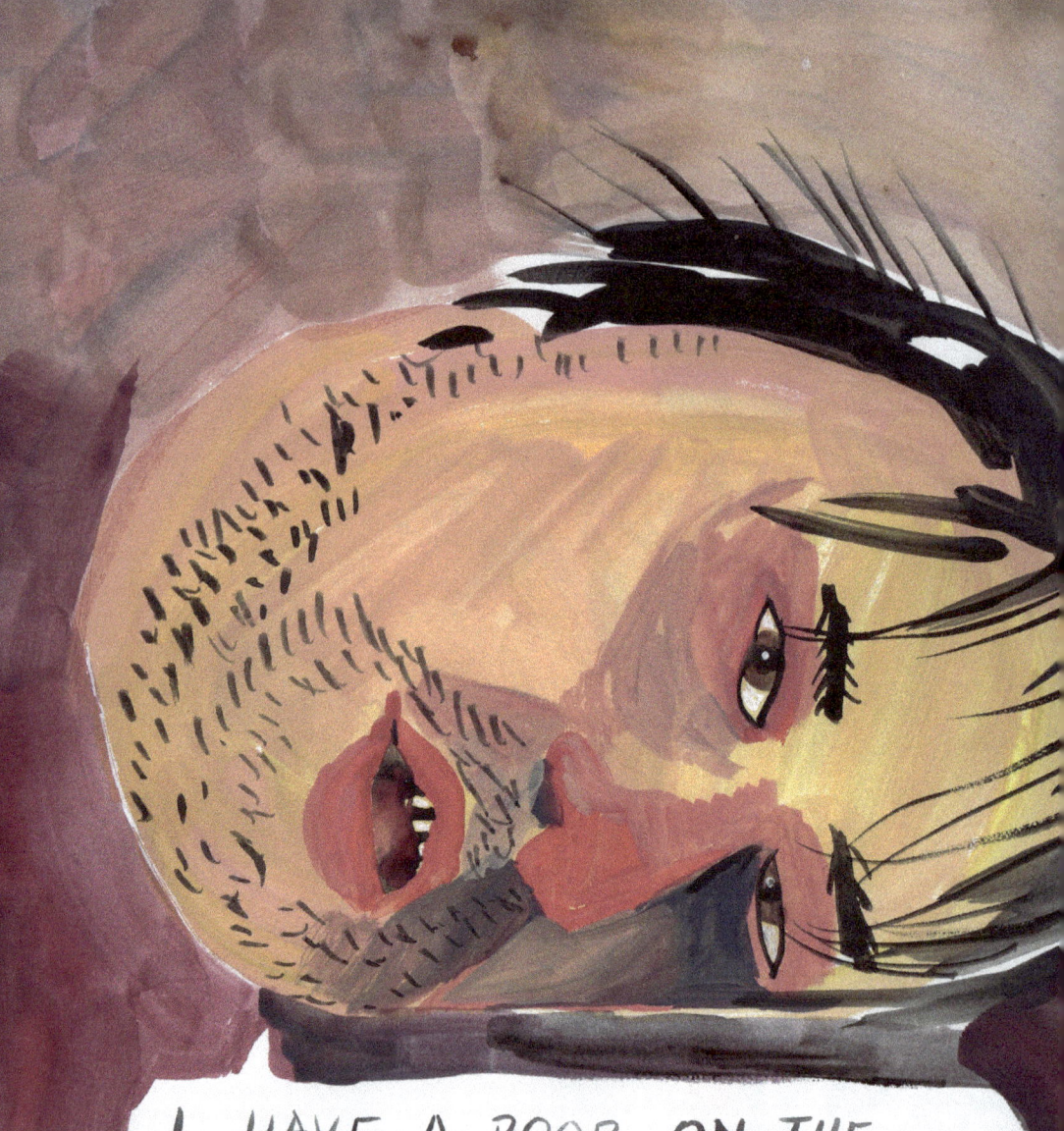

COMMON ᴺᴼᴺ SENSE

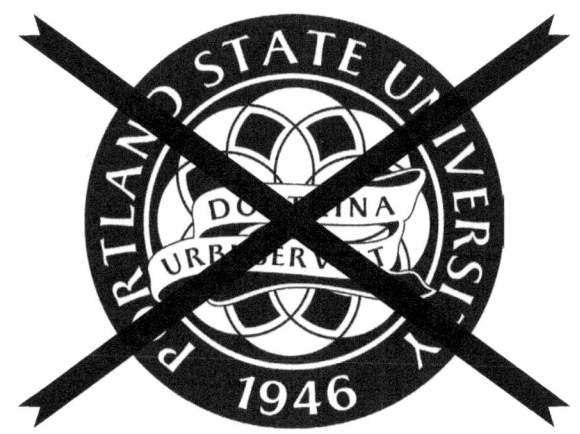

RANTS ON PERVERSITY AND TECHNOLOGY

OR

A CONFUSED CHORUS OF IDEAS
PECKING AWAY IN MY HEAD

FLESH
WALRUS

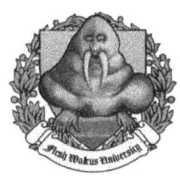

get in the steamroom NOW! it's time to discuss philosophy

CLASSICS

THE IMPORTANCE OF SMUT

OBSCENITY EXISTS ONLY IN THE MINDS THAT DISCOVER IT AND CHARGE OTHERS WITH IT!

ROMANS XIV: 14:
"I know and am persuaded by the Lord Jesus that there is nothing unclean of itself, but to him that esteemeth anything to be unclean, to him it is unclean.

ADULTS NEED OBSCENE LITERATURE, AS MUCH AS CHILDREN NEED FAIRY TALES, AS A RELIEF FROM THE OPPRESSIVE FORCE OF CONVENTION.

(break to online shop for sunglasses)

THE MOST INSISTENT QUESTION PUT TO THE WRITER OF "OBSCENE" LITERATURE IS:

Why did you have to use such language?

WRITING IS A VITAL AND MYSTERIOUS FORCE! AND I AM NOTHING BUT A VESSEL FOR GOD'S SMUT TO SHINE THROUGH! WHAT KIND OF WORLD DO WE LIVE IN

THAT FICTIONAL SAUCY CONCUPISCENCE IS MORE OBSCENE THAN THE FACT THAT WE PAY TAXES TO PUT HUMAN BEINGS IN SOLITARY CONFINEMENT!!!!!!!?????????

(I am very tired and my geriatric bedtime -- 8:30pm -- is rapidly approaching)

WHAT IS OBSCENE THEN? THE WHOLE FABRIC OF LIFE AS WE KNOW IT TODAY! I BELIEVE THAT WHAT WE CALL MORALITY IS MERELY A FORM OF MADNESS!!!!

In the Gospel of Mary, Christ says

THERE IS NO SUCH THING AS SIN!

Also, the disciples, in their quest for the divine, should follow no authorities, heed no rules, but simply **look within themselves**. Having delivered these lessons, Jesus departs, leaving his disciples quaking with fear.

NO SIN? NO RULES? NOTHING BUT DISCOVERING THE DIVINE WITHIN YOURSELF?

If they teach these doctrines, they might end up getting killed, like him.

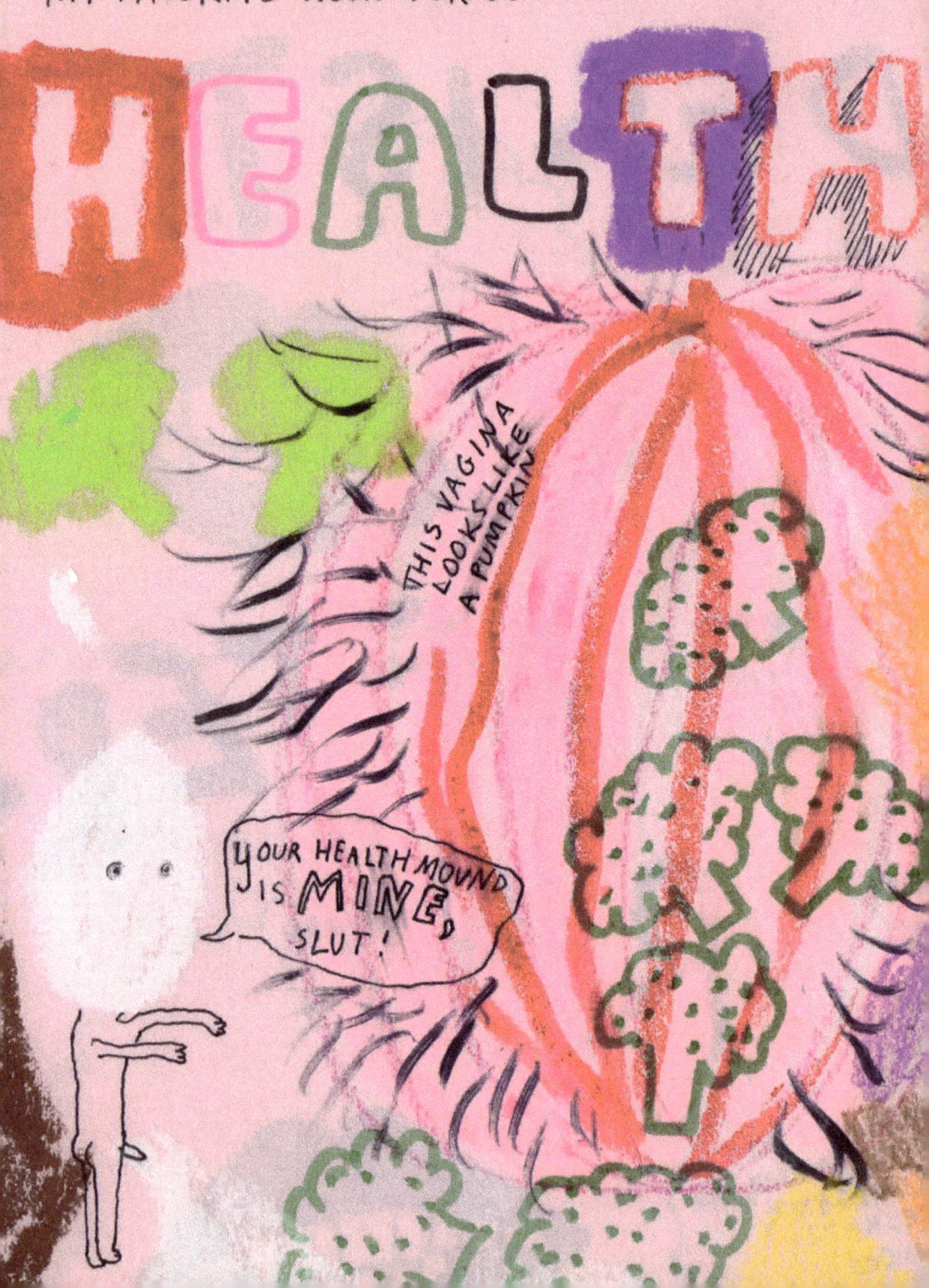

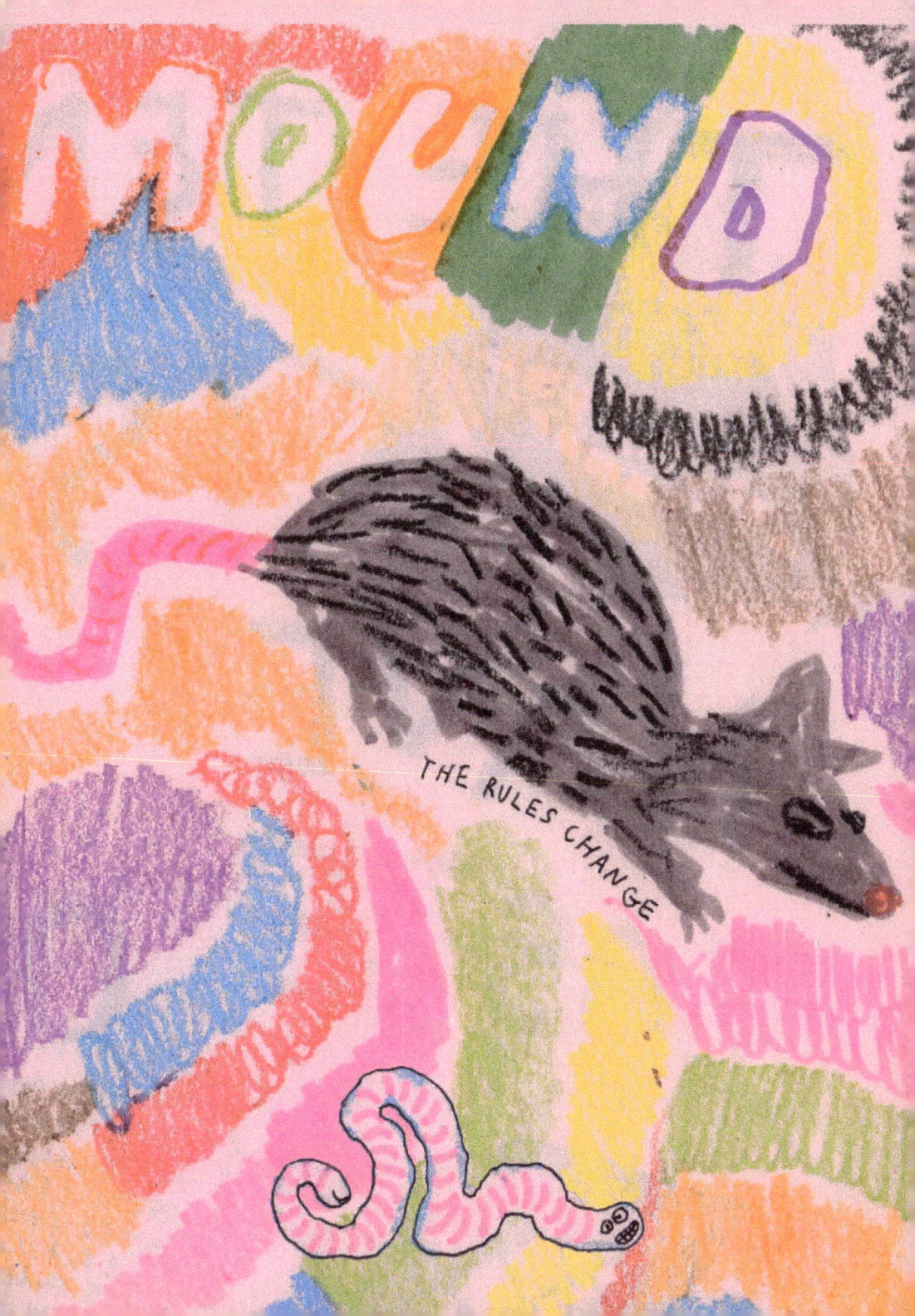

re: the milk hole, things that aren't fungible,
    rescuing words from extinction via
    arduous anfractuous perennial progress
    aka the story of my life as a worm
    eating wild wings
      after midnight.

Dear

Kafka hated letters, yet he wrote so many of them. This is just a brief distraction, a procrastination from an assignment to write about my navel. I am alone in my studio, in a dissolute daze. People are so disappointing (the disappointment is in direct proportion to my self-pity). There is a law , the social law of gravity: the nights your soul is wimpering before the bleak vast nothingness it is guarenteed that nobody will return your calls there will be no spontaneous knock on the door no sweetness unfurled by an admirer... just your own muddled thoughts, microwavable popcorn, and ashes. but when you feel effervescent, when the overwhelming fog of death breaks and the overwhelming feeling flips so that the coin faces life, and i look upon the world as if for the first time, like a baby who finds endless entertainment in the ceiling... that is when the good news arrives, the email from a prospective paramour, & you feel like you have too many friends & must protect your solitude...

FRAGMENTS

Equal parts philosophical and spiritual

> grieving the death of the
> long-term illusion that
> something outside of myself
> can fix me.

I want to shed my stuff, my art, even my identity.
It is too heavy for me.
— my diary

When it snows, I get a boner.
— Mark Leidner

Life expands in proportion to one's courage.
— Anais Nin

Jesus was a Black lesbian.*
— Kevin Carter

*Upon fact checking:

◆ AI Overview

No, Jesus was not a Black lesbian, and there is no evidence to support this claim:

Do you touch anything more than you touch your phone?–

Do you dine with your phone?
Do you poop with your phone?
Do you ask Google existential questions?
Do you sleep with your phone beside you?
Do you ever leave your phone behind?
Do you see the world through its bloodless lens?
Have you ever looked at an exquisite sunset and thought it looks just like a screen saver?

In an economy of visibility, attractiveness equals worth.–

One's curated images, whether or not they have to do with reality, are the first criteria by which one is judged on social media. Is the perfect profile photo what will preserve the human species? Will personalities be dictated by "likes?"

What is this tension I feel in the presence of another body?–

We can seemingly tell each other anything in the absence of our bodies – hence the appeal of the confession booth. But in person, the specter becomes all too human, one wishes they could cower behind the screen sending kisses that never reach their destination* (i.e. emojis). We forget the strange

*Franz Kafka: *Written kisses don't reach their destination, rather they are drunk on the way by the ghosts.*

brutal hopelessly neurotic loving creature hidden inside that fearfully real flesh. The disembodied person has no impact, no gravity, no *punctum*. The screen is an echo chamber and sounding board for our thoughts. We have control. We control who we talk to. We can end the conversation at will. We can control the way we look. We can have diarrhea while revealing what happened to us that fateful day in the basement. Flesh communicates unicity. We are also not one. We exist in separate skin suits, we see through different eyes, we look different from our pictures, we have a big pimple on the sebaceous side of our nose, we have dill in our teeth and nervous tics and pheromones and shit in our cracks.

I feel like there's a hymen between myself and the world.—

We must allow our sense of reality to be broken in order to be enlarged by the Other. Like the sheath of a seed, nothing can grow without breaking. The virtual world exists as an anodyne, while reality is a violent tear. Transformation is married to hurt.

And don't you want to transform…

The technology with which a seed can transform into a 2,000 year old redwood tree that is in itself is an intricate ecosystem, the technology which can transform the sperm squirming in some viscid gunk into a universe containing universes – a body – is a sophisticated system leagues beyond iphones and laptops and devices which are a shitty version of our brain, a bloodless ersatz eyeball.

Images do not bleed.

Let us gently shock ourselves by becoming something other than what we expected or even wanted.–

How many times have you forced your face into a pantomime of joviality while dying inside?
Yet when we see images of people enacting joy and superiority we mistake it for the real thing, we yearn for this fantastical tableau. We think we are living the wrong life. We mistake the right way to be for a picture in a feed.

Reality doesn't look like anything but itself.–

In a society that prizes speed and efficiency,
human connection is less valuable than connecting to WiFi.
For love, in all its variegations, is a terrible distraction.
It slows us down. It forces us to stop and feel.

We ask our phones to diagnose, solve, record, remember, direct, entertain, matchmake, predict, communicate... perhaps the better question is, what don't we turn to our smart phones for?

Who hasn't experienced the frail sort of happiness that depends on a notification?

Art's inoculation against the Image World lies in the recognition that we are incessantly creating. Every thought is an act of imagination. Art is self-defense against the dominant imagination, the spurious hallucination that purports to be axiomatic reality.

Otherwise we live in a matrix of advertisements in an earnest quest dictated by fashionable lies. Such is the fate of a feeble imagination.

> But eventually I want to create a system where I am offline and away from devices most of the time
>
> Tech autocracy and surveillance really bothers me
>
> You'll have to sext me via pigeon

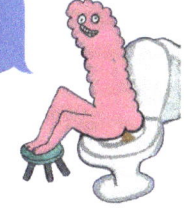

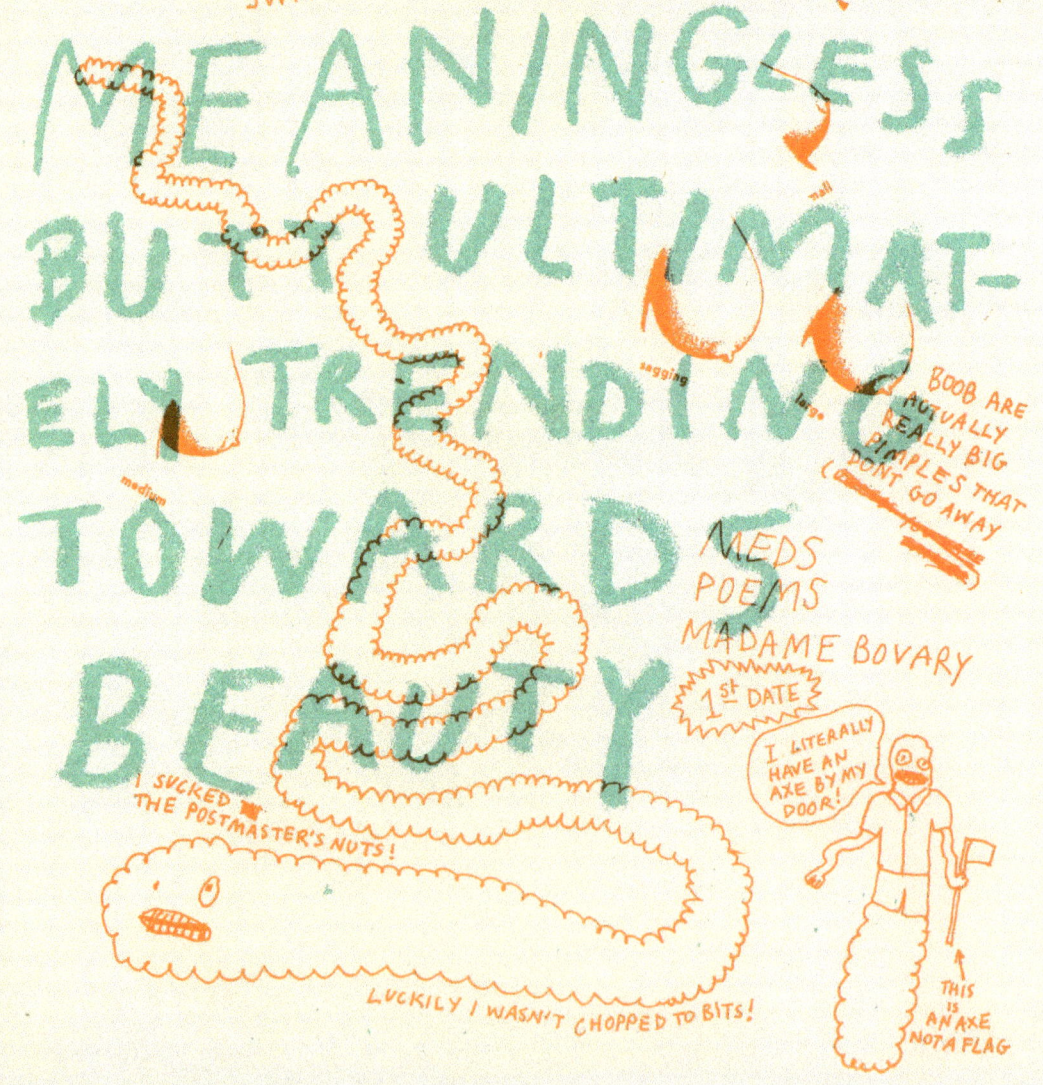

It irks me that carrying devices has become a safety issue. Prevailing wisdom warns against meeting new people in corporeal simplicity; being careful = augmenting myself with a fully charged phone and sharing my location with a trusted friend. What if I get raped/ dismembered/ refrigerated/ robbed/ rolled up in a carpet in the back of a truck/ immured in a basement with a bed made of plastic bags filled with crunchy dead leaves, doomed to watch Exorcist III ad infinitum with my unhinged captor... or, what if I get LOST? – fear prevails.

What if I don't know where I am, and I'm late to responding to so and so's texts, thereby indicating that I take her for granted and disrespect her time, or I'm late for a zoom meeting, or neglect messaging any number of my 118 Hinge matches,* only two of which I'll actually meet?

With every passing moment of Time Not Optimized (my riposte to Proust's *In Search of Lost Time)*, I am not living up to my Full Potential!!!!!!!! and I'm falling behind on my endless list of meaningless obligations, not one of which is to just breathe.

Could time scarcity have anything to do with the proliferation of time made visible, like the ghost of an ex

---

*I say this with Christ-like humility.

that relentlessly haunts your thoughts? Always checking the weather, the need to know which animal poops cubes NOW, the overstimulated brain sizzling on a frying pan of incessant correspondence, always knowing every bad thing that's happened everywhere at all times; a brain infested with the scabies of doom-consciousness.

And I wonder why I have difficulty trusting myself; in technology I trust; there are cameras in the hallway, so if you kill me, my mom will find out.

My intuition is sotto voce.

When I lock my phone in my P.O. box and go about my day with the intention of being in uninterrupted life, I must persevere through a feeling of agitation like a captive animal in the first hours of its domestication; the number of times I check my phone measures the depth of my anxiety, yet I rely upon those pinpricks of connection to manage the anxiety those pinpricks induced.

And I feel as though an invisible umbilical cord is tugging me back into the womb. The internet is a womb. A dark space where the external world ceases to exist and you can endlessly amass evidence that reinforces your intransigent beliefs. You can safely suck on your glass teat while gormandizing trendy snacks with packaging designed by the best artists of our generation who otherwise would not be able to afford their well-lit ikea-furnished cells. Your suicidal snacking habits are cushioned with the sophistry that by putting your faith in cauliflower pretzels, you are superior to the diabolical Dorito bingers. Your cauliflower pretzels support blacklivesmatter, with every crunch you are stopping asian hate and advocating for gay rights and legalized abortion. Your snacks and sweatpants liquidate beliefs and values and causes and cultures and identities such that when I say my name is Ashley Yang-Thompson, I am reaping my Yang-ness for its promotional potential.

Ashley

yang

yang

fire

of

thy

loins

thompson

WHERE DO YOU BEGIN WHEN YOU ARE DROWNING IN DESPAIR?

You begin with Goya's drowning dogs during his *Black Paintings* phase. You begin with Camus saying *there is no love of life without despair of life*. You begin with that memorable question Noriko asks her sister at the end of Ozu's *Tokyo Story*: *Isn't life disappointing?* You begin remembering what a totally ordinary septuagenarian told you over a chai latte, something like, *if you're driving across the country and your car breaks down, you don't start from where you began, you start from where you broke down*, i.e. there is no going backwards in art or in life. You begin exactly where you are. You begin with having nothing to say. You begin with four minutes and thirty three seconds of silence. You begin with Bruce Nauman filming nothing happening in his studio because *nothing is something*.

The Zero-Dopamine Lifestyle

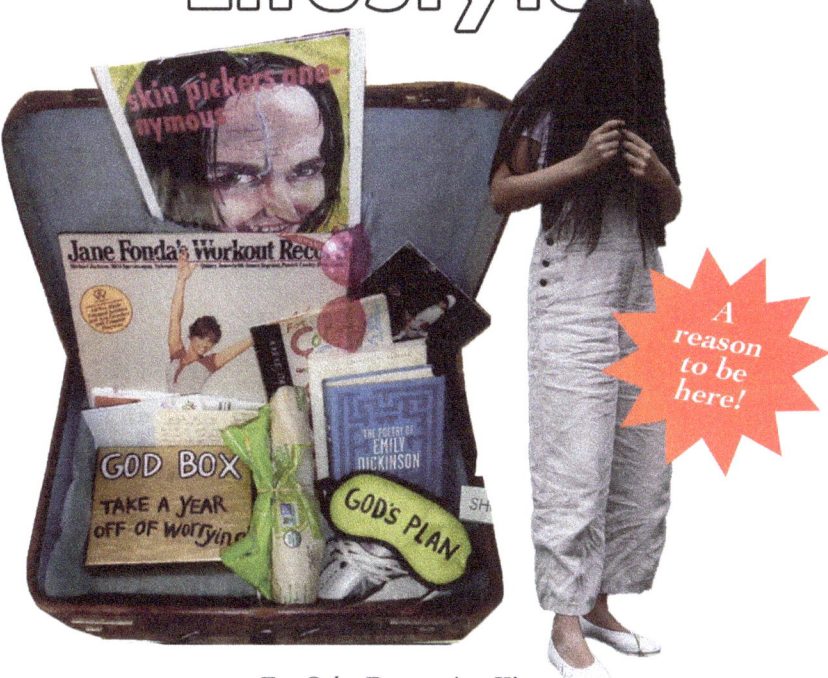

For Sale: Depression Kit

Jane Fonda's Original Workout, heating pad (inhuman califaction), heartfelt letters, Skin Pickers Anonymous flyer, rose–tinted myopia, a lasting experience of God, aphorisms, chunky childhood photos, the dregs of my housemate's tortilla chips, suitcase. This depression kit literally saved my life.

SHOPPER'S GUIDE   ISSUE OF JULY   SERVING THE TRI-STATE COMMUNITY

An Aesthetics of Sculpting with Flesh[*]

Your nature, princess, is indeed noble and true;
but events fester, and divinity is sick.
— Euripides

Sometimes I look at my past work (a dissonant experience) and wonder, *What was I thinking?* I wasn't thinking, I was creating. And my method was corybantic and unedited (just like my pubic hair). As a Very Young Person, I was reacting to a society that distorts the body into a moral issue. On hot summer days in my unairconditioned domicile, my male housemates could walk around shirtless without a second thought. For me to do the same would be a monumental exercise in overcoming double-consciousness, as well as potentially dangerous and illegal if I exposed my chthonic nipples to the public. The project of my twenties was to push against the systems I was born into by using my body as my medium, my effluvia as a provocation to the puppet-masters-at-large.

I was censored everywhere I went, despite the unoriginality of my defiant gestures (the beginning of art history – Venus of Willendorf – is a buxom female nude). The more pushback I received, the more I felt an urge to stand my

---

[*]Mike Kelley, *Foul Perfection: Notes on Caricature* (1989)

ground – who says I should be ashamed? Who says this is bad art? Who determines what's good? Can't I decide who I am? If my art is sexually arousing, isn't that YOUR problem? As Jesus advised, *If your right eye causes you to stumble, gouge it out and throw it away.*

It troubled me that my art was often interpreted as a kind of pornography, and I struggled with my lack of control over the fantasies that were projected onto me, all the while writing poems like:

i need to buy a pink and turquoise mermaid sea shell ruffle
swimsuit so that i can look like a
really really hot
asian
baby
prostitute

I felt disassociated from the content of my work. The shamelessness expressed in my art was not, I felt, connected to reality. As Louise Bourgeois wrote, *In real life, I identify with the victim, in my art I am the murderer.* Art was the sphere where I made the rules, where my own intentions and perspectives reigned, a thoroughly *imagined* alternate universe where there was nothing inherently weird or even immodest about taking off all my clothes and peeing on somebody's foot to make a point about colonialism.

Who's Buried Here?

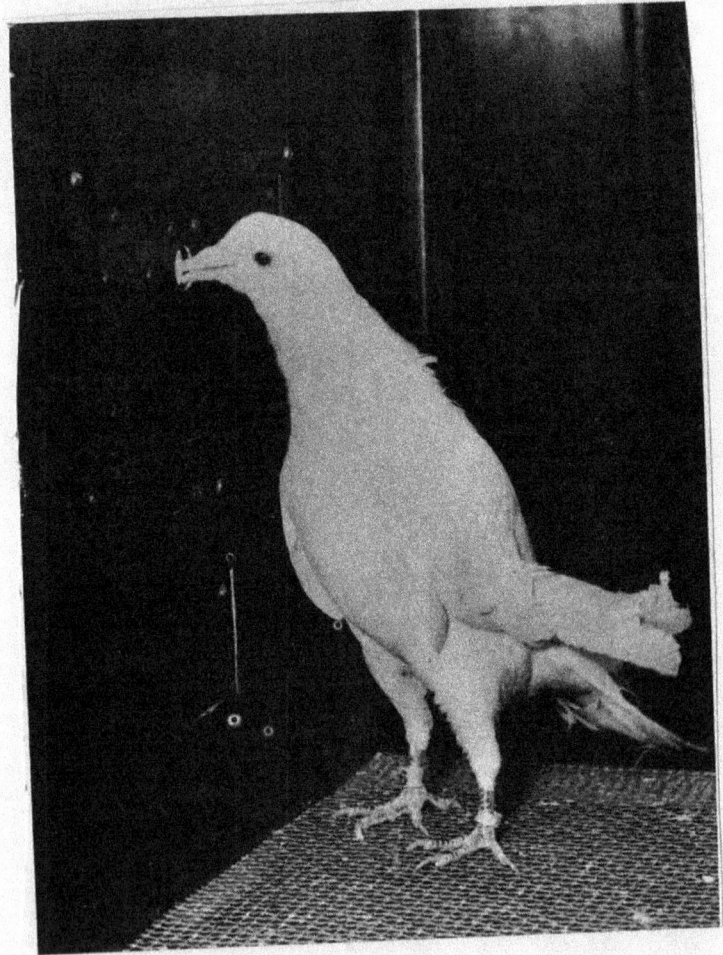

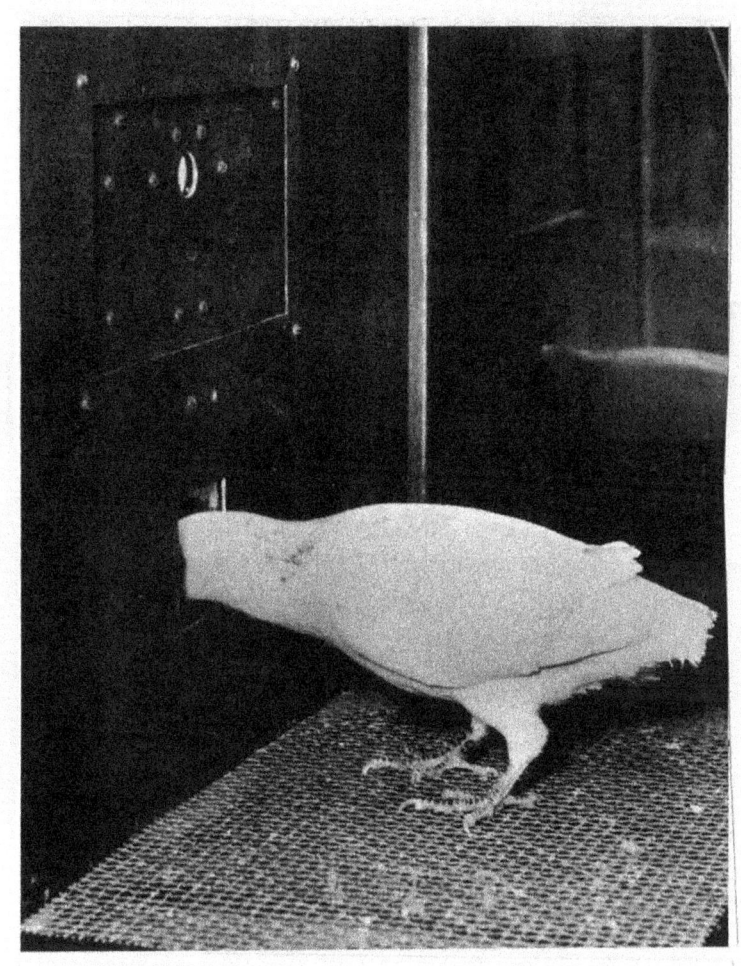

Chinese child prostitutes.

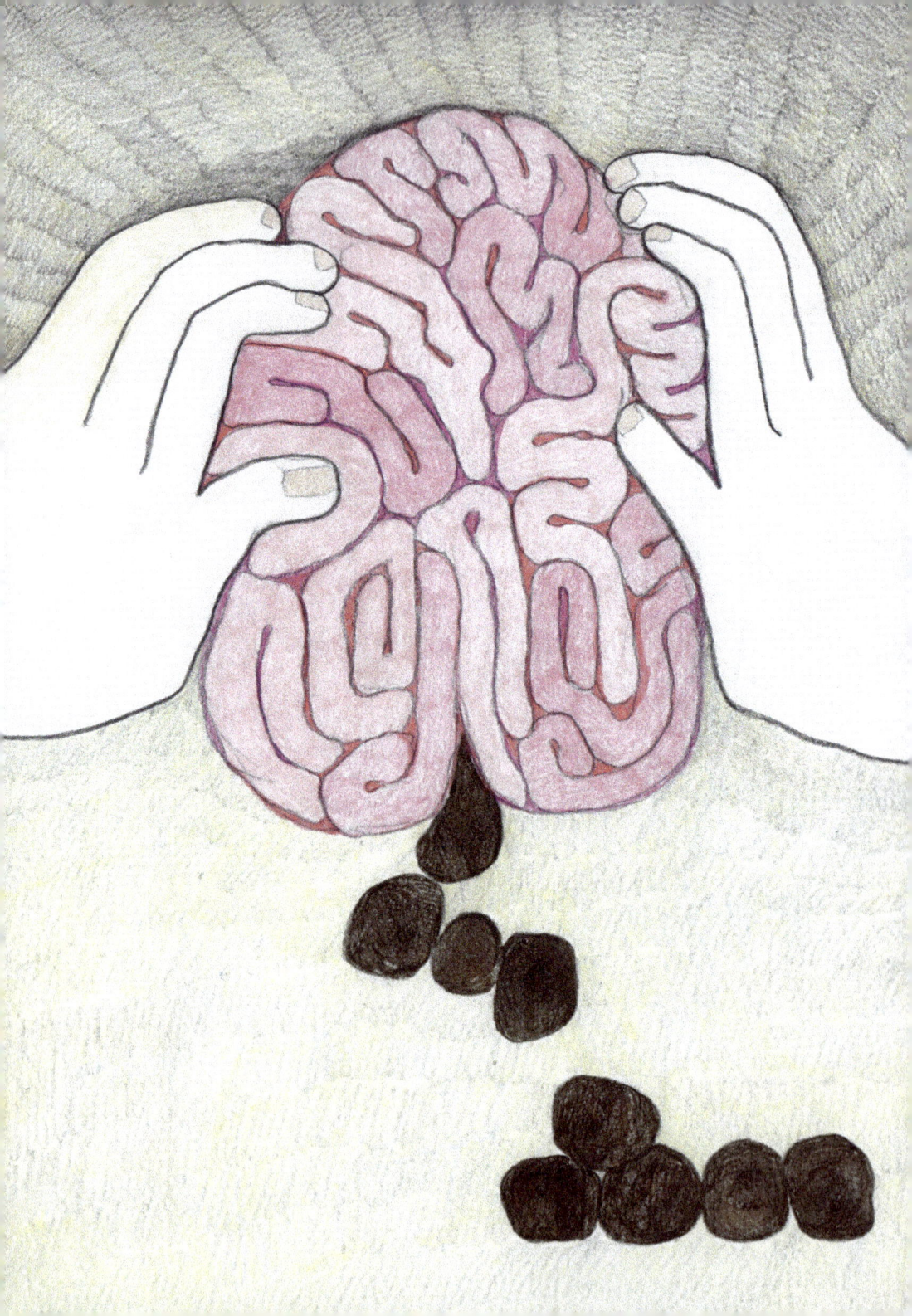

Artist's Block as A Way of Life

I hate writing. I have nothing interesting to say. Or maybe I have something interesting to say, but I definitely don't have the energy to say it. I hate myself. I better go waste my food stamps buying shots of charcoal at my local health foods store.

I want the words to pour out of me in one fell swoop, to drop from the bowels of my genius like a ripe fruit, but instead my ideas have to be forcibly squeezed out of my mind's anus like constipated pebbles. "Repeat after me, I am a vessel for God's light to shine through," says the soothing white lady from the youtube affirmation video. "I am a vessel for God's light to shine through," I tell myself. And then add, "Be patient. After all, the Koran was revealed to Muhammad over the course of 23 years."

My work is not timely, it is timeless. I make work for the children of the Earth 6 generations from now, which is why I draw so many pimples, so that one day, mark my words, teenagers will be rubbing sticks of butter all over their faces, praying for a fat zit to erupt on prom night.

Which reminds me of a dream my friend once told me, about being covered in huge cystic pimples. Like the circumference-of-a-mayonnaise-jar-huge. So he wrapped a belt around his stomach. He pulled it tighter and tighter and tighter, watching the cysts pulse in response. He could barely breathe. He gave the belt one final squeeze, and suddenly all 100 pimples burst at once, oozing everywhere. He said it was so satisfying and disgusting, every sexual experience since that moment has been a vain attempt to recreate that feeling.

Goddamnit. I don't want to write about pimples.
Why can't I ever write the thing I want to write? The kind of thing that illuminates my entirely ordinary existence with a strange intrigue, as if every moment without exception were a necessary puzzle piece to a picture beyond comprehension but which I can glimpse fleetingly in moments of inspiration.* The kind of thing that makes you laugh so hard that you cry, or cry so hard that you laugh. The kind of thing that makes you want to be kinder to the asshole driver who flipped you off because maybe his son shot himself a few years ago, probably not, but maybe.

---

*The perspicuous white light of insight; relief from the endlessnessnessness of the importunate inner monologue.

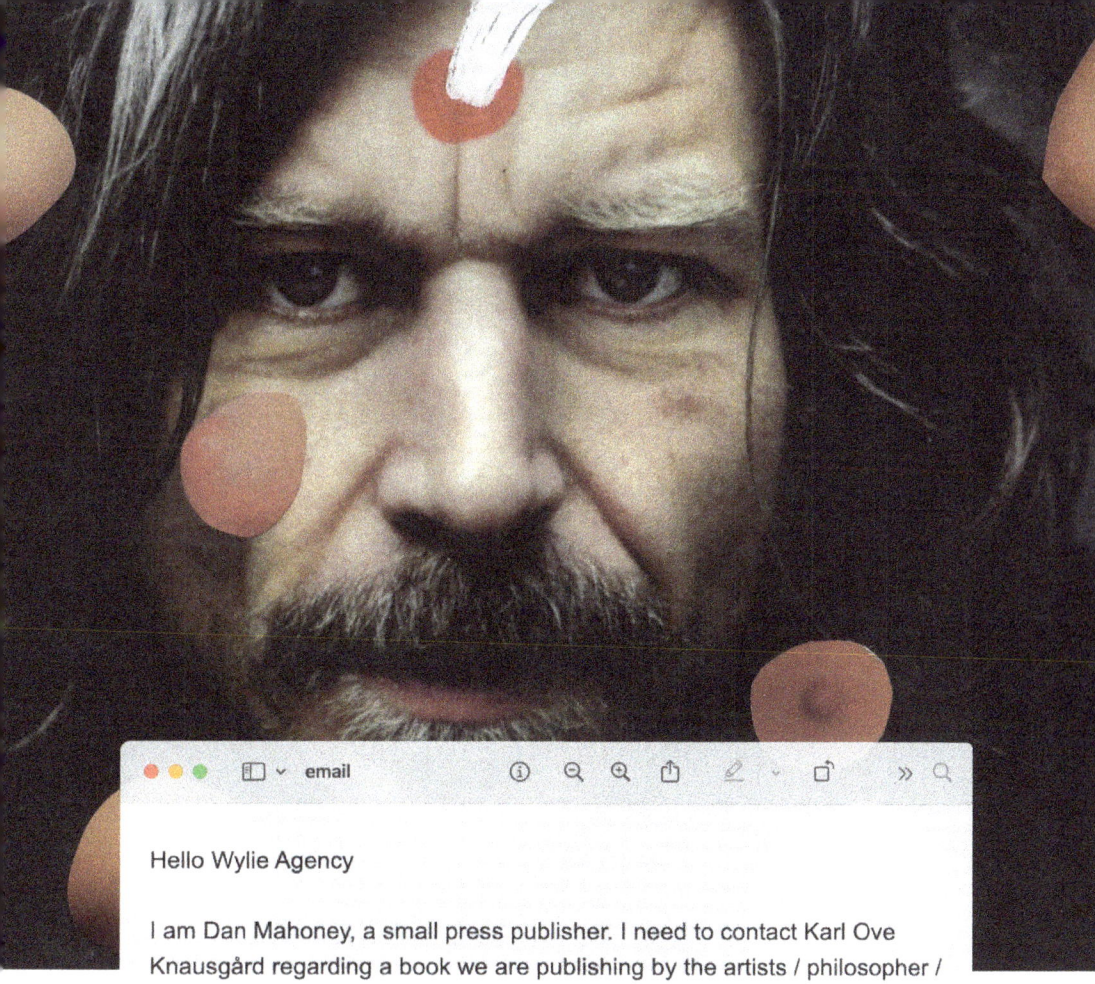

Hello Wylie Agency

I am Dan Mahoney, a small press publisher. I need to contact Karl Ove Knausgård regarding a book we are publishing by the artists / philosopher / literary savant Ashly Yang-Thompson. Ashley's latest book, *Still Worm*, is dedicated to Karl Ove and we would like to:

1. see if Karl Ove could send us a headshot and a blurb for *Still Worm*
2. see if Karl Ove could facetime with Ashley for the betterment of humanity
3. see if Karl Ove would like a copy of the book when published

Please let me know how to proceed.
all best
--
Dan Mahoney
Editor in Chief
Bateau Press / Bateau Lit Mag

"A poem shouldn't be

Maybe I can finish this book
if I stop online shopping for clogs
~Ashley Yang-Thompson

today i will judge nothing that occurs

Dear Ashley,

You write because it is one of the few natural sources of dopamine you have left.

You don't write as much as you'd like to, because everything that doesn't involve draping yourself across soft surfaces feels like a slog, although every once and a while you find that you can write with half your face pressed against a pillow, drooling. But this is an ergonomically unsound way to pursue the little daily miracles of your life, which you can consecrate through writing.

You write because – let's be honest – nobody makes you laugh more than you. You write to experience a fuller range of feelings, to feel a kind of heaviness that grounds you to this Earth, to emerge with a lightness because somehow even when all the psychiatric prescriptions fail – which they typically do – writing burns off the fog. Not always, but often enough. When you write, you are here, not detached and dissociated – which is the way you live your life, but not the way you write it.

In life, you are – contrary to all your progressive beliefs – unable to break out of that narrow – impossibly narrow – space of what's acceptable. You are unable to color outside of the lines of the systems and archetypes you were born into.

But art has kept your soul alive because in art you don't have to be the sub. In art, you can awaken the protean part of you that is buried deep within your crazy skin suit.

You can drift towards the dark core you're running from.

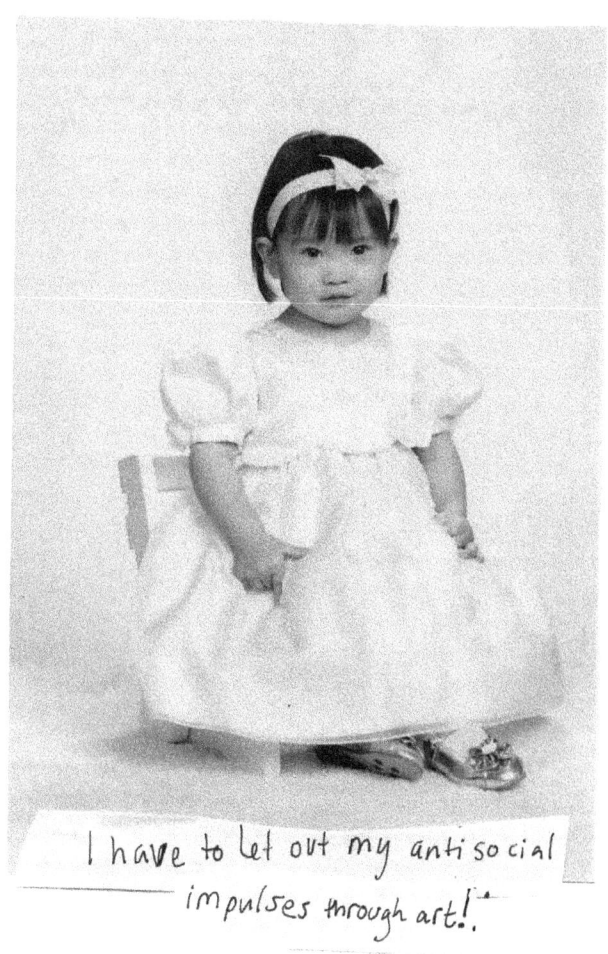

"I have to let out my antisocial impulses through art!"

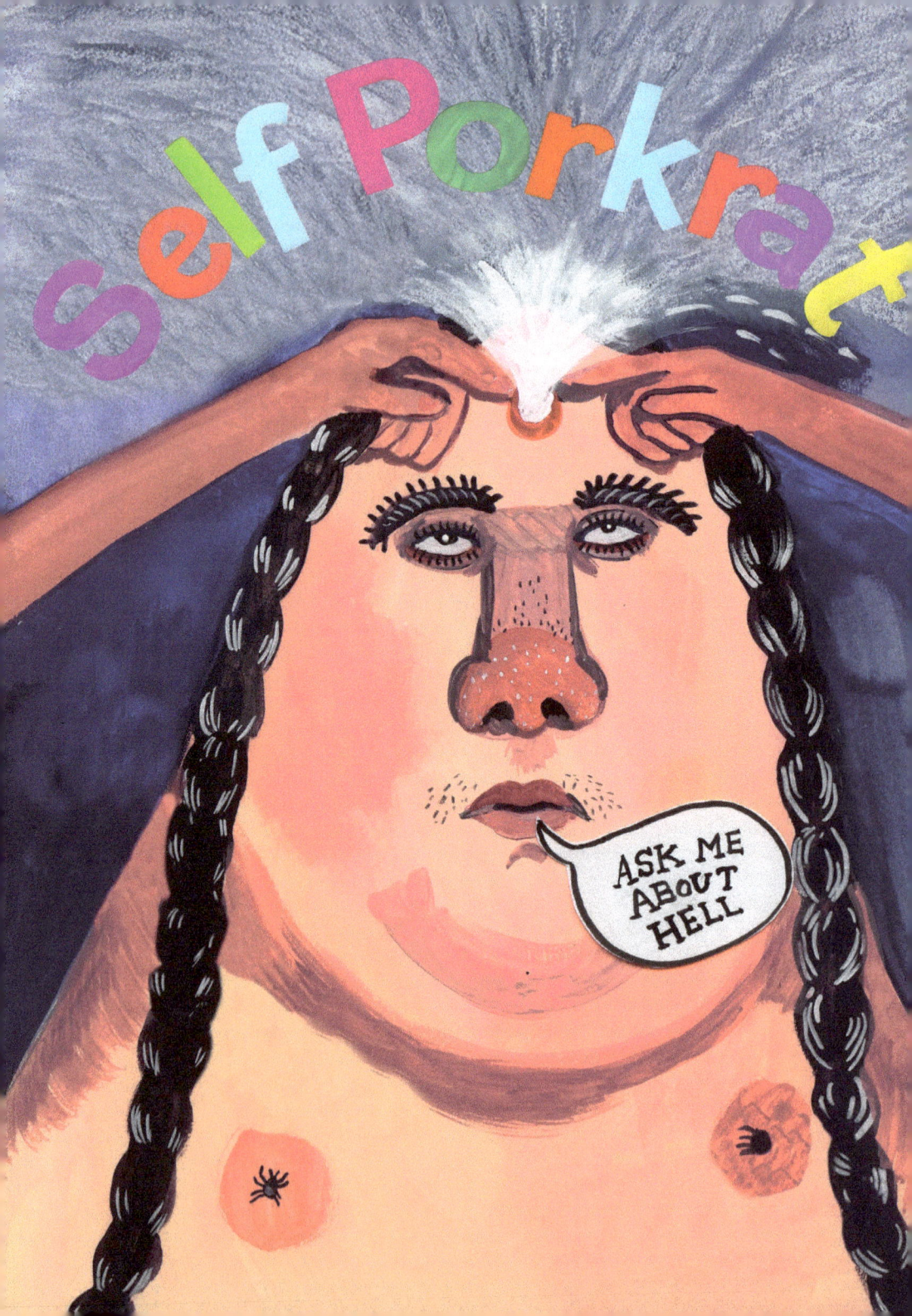

At the age of six I wanted to be a crab. At seven I wanted to be a broadway star. At nineteen I wanted to be a famous artist/millionaire. At twenty I wanted to be Jesus Christ. At twenty-three I wanted to be the expanding universe. Actually, I mostly just wanted to be a really really hot frighteningly erudite asian baby prostitute. And my ambition has been steadily ~~atomizing~~ growing ever since.

I am thirty-two years old, and all the way down to the hole in my butt, I am a different person.

I no longer aspire to look like an anime porn-boy. Though I have been known to dance fiercely with aerobic technique, Broadway has eluded me. I have prayed morning and night on my knees without knowing precisely for what, but I am not a milestone of human consciousness. I have contemplated suicide countless times, but I no longer think about it. I want only two things: first, to gracefully ~~endure~~ *endear** the ordeal of loving; and second, to grow old – to become a majestic hag with drooping breasts that sway in sync to the pulse of my own integrity.

---

*Endear is, etymologically, "to make dear." To paraphrase the meditation instructor Vinny Farrago, "Rather than suffer patiently without yielding (i.e. to endure), how do we take whatever is happening, and make it beloved?"

Some Peripatetic Thoughts on Hell

Which way I fly is Hell; myself am hell! cries Satan in Milton's *Paradise Lost.*

For the better part of my twenties, I've had writer's block and artist's block, and the thought of being home alone typing on a rainy winter's night fills me with anticipated loneliness and the sensation that my chest is a clenched fist. I like to imagine myself as urbane, but in reality my face is adorned with pimple patches and I am listening to the crunchy chants of Krishna Das because the emptiness of my apartment (metonym for my soul) is terrifying.

Nietzsche wrote that *the path to one's own heaven always leads through the voluptuousness of one's own hell.* I remember looking up the word *enfer*, which was defined in the *French English Dictionary* as *hell (an uncomfortable situation).* I love that parenthetical statement. It says so much about the impersonal, hyperbolic nature of the mind. This hell I am experiencing – whether it be losing someone dear to me or

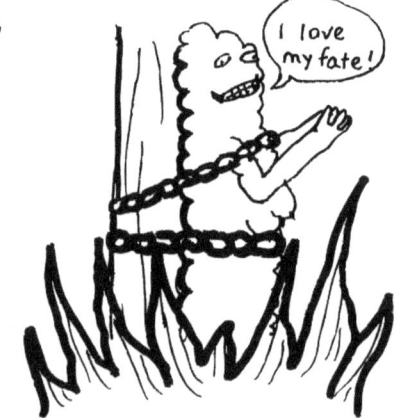

the dissolution of an ideal or some other psychic abortion – is just *an uncomfortable situation.* No need to add concentric circles of hell by unskillfully picking at my literal and figurative pustules.

For Christmas, my brother gave me a photo album of pictures he found when he was clearing out my dad's house in 2022. I spent the rest of the day in tears. How did I get here? In the confused chronology in which life is experienced, wasn't I eleven years old the day before yesterday? And wasn't my dad cremated just a few months after his unexpected diagnosis? And isn't it urgent that I start living my own life and inhabiting this meatsack before I, too, return to dust?

Maya Angelou said, *It is a privilege to cry honest tears*; it is a privilege to let go of something beautiful and meaningful and utterly – *write it!* – irreplaceable. In the *Ninth Duino Elegy*, Rilke writes, *Your most sacred tenet is Death the intimate Friend… Look! I am living…. Superabundant existence wells in my heart.* To grieve fully is to remain in my body, to stay with the uncomfortable situation, to not shutter the formidable wound with a mindless palliative. To honor Death and loss as my intimate Friends. To insist on being here for the *full catastrophe* – and eucatastrophe – *of life.* With the velocity of a constipated earthworm, I let go and let go and let go.

STILL WORM

A week or two before his death, my father summoned me to a formal colloquy. Looking up at him in his elevated wheelchair, he might as well have been seated on a throne. He had not yet lost the magical authority he held over me as a child. He told me I was lost; he hoped that I would "find my way." I already knew that I was lost. After all, what had my artistic ambitions amounted to? Living in a moldy basement? A series of minimum-wage jobs and fleeting romantic relationships? Chronic lethargy and a medley of ineffective prescription medications? I reacted defensively. I accused him of being like my mother, who continued to insist that I get an MBA so that I could fulfill her dream of buying a condo near Bloomingdales.

My father has been dead for over two years, the reality of which I have been slow to metabolize. Soon after he died, I wrote:

Might I get to know you better in your absence?
I keep thinking of monolithic mother trees
and this one episode of Planet Earth *that talked*
about parasitic vines that wind their way around
the mother and slowly strangle it to death
and how this transition creates space for its seeds to grow
because in its immensity the mother has deprived its offspring
of water and sunlight.

Buried beneath strata of resentment and dysfunction, my poem exhumed what I unconsciously knew: the inimical patriarch of my childhood was a strange, loving, brutal creature, *just like me.* (Perhaps, if Nietzsche were to write a sequel to *Beyond Good and Evil* for today's therapeutic era, it would be entitled, *Beyond Mom and Dad.*) I didn't come to this understanding gracefully; I regressed before gradually *suffering into truth.* No longer "chill," if a friend cancelled plans with me, I would break down in a primal fit of heaving sobs. I contemplated suicide multiple times a day. I felt the overwhelming need to sacrifice my life to prove how much his life meant to me. I purposely put myself in danger as if to confront my dead parent – *How could you leave me? Who will protect me now?*

Dear Dad,
Who will I call when I don't know what to do,
which is always?
Will I really never hear you say,
"I'm in a meeting, call you back in 5 minutes" again?

I recently renamed this book *STILL WORM.* The title comes from Nietzsche's *Thus Spoke Zarathustra: You have evolved from worm to man, but much within you is still worm.* As fond as I am of Nietzsche, I believe there is much to gain from what I call *the worm way.*

The worm way is hermeneutic; something numinous courses beneath the surface of things. When infused with sacredness, reading is a method of living meaningfully, feeling deeply, and complicating narratives that are suspiciously easy to accept. Writing is my reading of the world. Perhaps Nietzsche's Übermensch is capable of writing the great American novel, but I am *still worm*. When I watch worms wriggle across the relatively vast expanse of a hiking trail, it's apparent they don't know where they're going but *they know where they're going.* Trusting in some intrinsic compass, they put their faith in the next inch. While thinking like a superman leads me to stultifying perfectionism, moving like a worm – one inch at a time – leads to a sentence.

In the ICU,
I did not know where you were,
your mouth a lonesome oval,
a respirator making an opera out of your breath,
needles everywhere, blood samples,
tubes and urostomy pouches and percutaneous endoscopic
gastronomy… I imagined you stuck in some desert between life
and death. I read you one of your favorite poems by T.S. Eliot,
and I swear you stirred at this line:

"The only wisdom we can hope to acquire
is the wisdom of humility: humility is endless."

Worms are telluric; they are *of the earth*. Fearlessly they burrow into the dark soil, and compost what is found there. This is the *endlessness* humility promises: an arduous anfractuous perennial progress. In *The Marriage of Heaven and Hell*, William Blake writes, *Improvement makes straight roads, but the crooked roads without/ Improvement, are roads of Genius.* Blake's straight road is the trajectory of career ladders and socially sanctioned milestones and self-help literature that promise Ultima Thule of permanent happiness. To quit the self-improvement trajectory is to encounter what is already here. By chipping away at the muck of myself, I am uncovering a very fine person who can meet my needs.

You have entered the deepest place in me
and when I close my eyes, I know that you're not gone.
I can find you in the fundamental particles of my being,
in the atoms that will outlast my own last breath.
You have made me larger,
and amplified what it means to be human.
It is physically impossible for you to die in my mind.
you exist
outside of time
& you are part of me
consoling and total
alive and well in the power
of what comes after.

What people are saying about
Still Worm

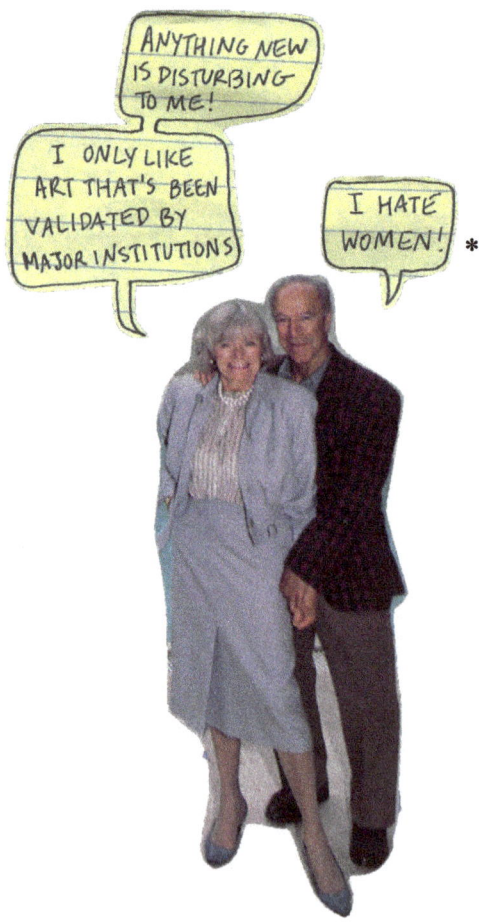

*We perceive that Ash Yang-Thompson threatens the social forms & norms that conceal the deforming structures of patriarchal power & domination.

Acknowledgments

First of all, I want to be clear that 99% of my art is plagiarized. But all of it is plagiarized by me.

My art is more or less my notes on life, and a thorough acknowledgment would include every person I've paid attention to, living and dead.

Here is an incomplete list of people to thank for ~~directly or indirectly assisting in my literary endeavors~~ laughing at my jokes: the baristas at Case Study Coffee Roasters, Guzman, Gabe Poucher, Júlia Sodré, Marina Reza, Lydia Shahan, Virginia McBride, Joaquin Golez, Nia Musiba, Ruby Bontrager, Kevin Sampsell, Tabitha Nikolai, Taravat Talepasand, Mikko Harvey, Michelle Kaplan, Adrian Ruth Williams, Loren Thompson and Mckinsey Carroll.

And thank you to Dan Mahoney at Bateau Press, for being the Silvia Beach of the 21st century.*

---

*Silvia Beach was the only person brave enough to originally publish the obscenely unhinged-now-canonical Ulysses. And, yes, in this analogy, I am James Joyce.

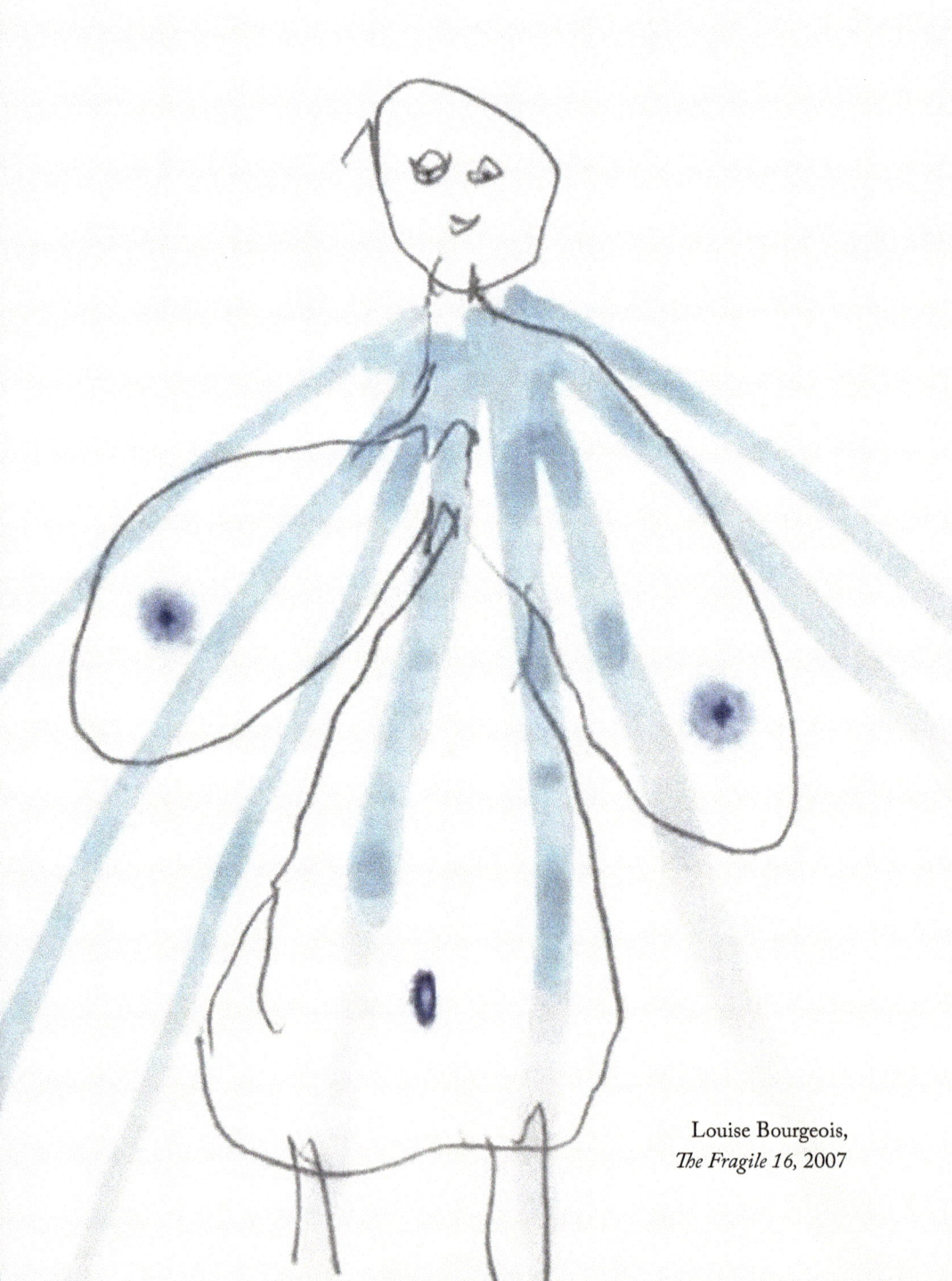

Louise Bourgeois,
The Fragile 16, 2007

Whatever we take ourselves to be we are not.

– Jacques Lacan

By refraining from rewriting this book, I honor the mystery (and surprise) of my own becoming. I honor the spontaneous, irreverent spirit in which *Still Worm* was written while acknowledging that this book now makes me cringe.

To me, an artist's individual works, however spellbinding, aren't nearly as compelling as the trajectory of art made over the course of a lifetime. If I were to remove one of Louis Bourgeois' booby spider drawings from her omnibus, it would be no different from the brilliantly undisciplined creations of my five year old niece. But seen as part of a labored, lifelong body of work, Bourgeois' genius shines as the author of her own language.

This little book is nothing more or less than an inch of the earthworm's journey. May it empower readers to write with process, not product, in mind.

Keep searching,

Ashley Yang-Thompson

THE WESTERN CANON

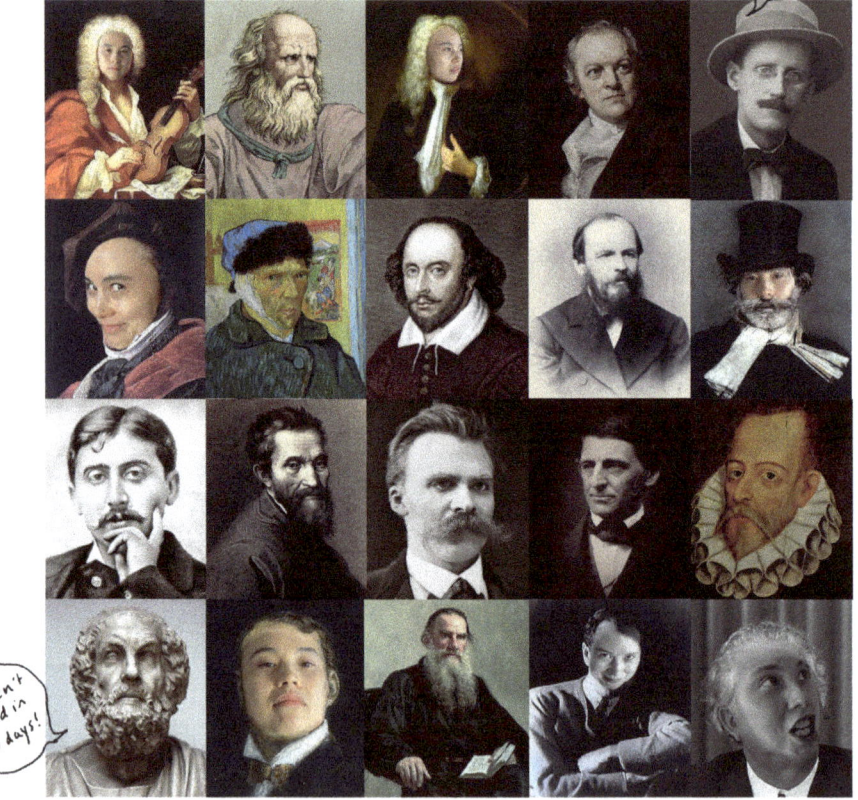

My poems are hysterical to me the first couple of times I read them; I can't help but laugh as I am reciting them. Then, gradually, I cease to laugh and lose enthusiasm for the poem. Can a poem wilt like a salad, best shared immediately? What makes a poem so good that it delivers with each recitation, and carries weight and meaning across a lifetime? A poem that transforms as you transform. The kind of poem where experience unlocks secret rooms within the poem you couldn't find before (as a callow sleuth). This is the kind of poem I must write: A CLASSIC.

About the Author

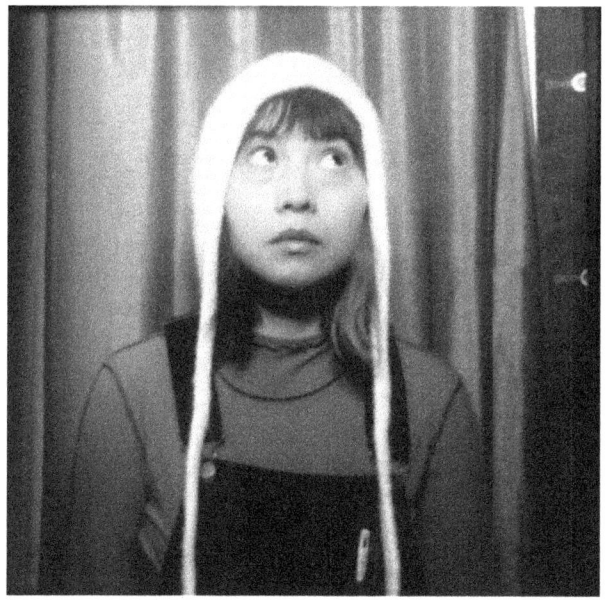

Ash Yang-Thompson is the author of *How to be the Worst Laziest Fattest Most Incontinent Piece-of-Shit in the world EVER* (Bateau Press, 2021) and the chapbook *Sky Mall* (above/ground press, 2020), which was written collaboratively with Mikko Harvey. She almost won a Pushcart Prize for her poem *White Fur Rug*. Ash currently lives in Portland, OR.

WHAT YOU ARE
HOLDING IN
YOUR HANDS
IS AN ORIGINAL
DESTINED TO
BECOME A
CLASSIC

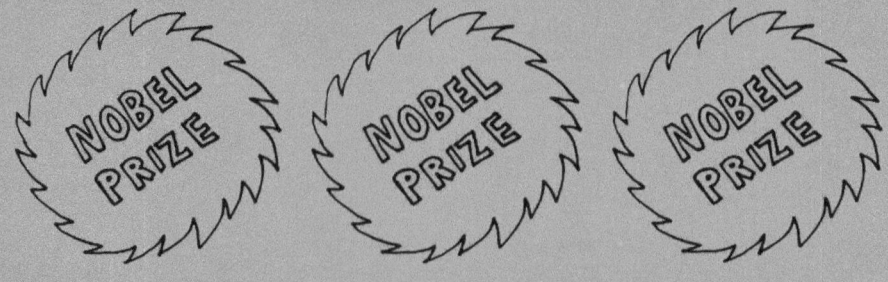